Language Education

DPH Education Series

Language Education

U K SINGH • K N SUDARSHAN

DISCOVERY PUBLISHING HOUSE
NEW DELHI-110002

Reprinted - 2019

First Published - 1996

ISBN: 978-81-7141-367-6

Language Education

Published by:

DISCOVERY PUBLISHING HOUSE PVT. LTD.
4383/4B, Ansari Road, Darya Ganj
New Delhi-110 002 (India)
Phone: +91-11-23279245, 23253475; 43596065
E-mail: discoverybooksindia@gmail.com
discoverypublishinghouse@gmail.com
web: www.discoverypublishinggroup.com

Printed at:
Infinity Imaging Systems
Delhi

Preface

The *DPH Education Handbook* has been created to provide access to information about contemporary topics in education. Practitioners and students at all levels in education have a need to know what is happening today, in addition to historical treatments within the literature.

Each chapter within the Handbook is designed to provide the user with needed "state-of-the-art" information as well as further sources of information. One of the significant features of each chapter is the inclusion of specific programmes, projects and activities so that the researcher can locate human resources as well as the literature.

The handbook will be of use to graduate and post graduate students in education and to practicing teachers, administrators, librarians and planners. The chapters and the further sources of information cited in each book should lead the reader to thousands of people and documents for either research or programme planning purposes.

An effort to achieve universal and effective education is based on a recognition of the rights of students to basic education that enables them to thrive in a complex society, as well as a realization the technological and economic growth is facilitated by increasing the numbers of students, even those with poor academic progresses, who are, in fact successful in learning. Thus, recent and current efforts improve education serve both private and social interests.

This series is addressed to administrators, planners and educators working in the field of education and training with a view to stimulating interest and attention in the areas of education and its related fields. It is also addressed to a growing number of teachers and instructors who will be practitioners in education and who will need to be acquainted with the modern aspects of educational practice and development. Many ideas, generalisations and discussions presented in this series should also prove useful to employing organisations committed to provide training facilities within their establishments—leading to effective mutual participation by institutions and organisations.

The editors wishes to thank the contributors, as well as those organizations that gave permission to publish their extracts, chapters etc.

Editors

Contents

1
Awareness of Language and School Learning

'Restricted' codes?

It is necessary to clear away a possible misunderstanding at the outset. We are not seeking to revive debate about the theory that certain languages used by some children are in some way intrinsically deficient, and that the children who use them are therefore in some way 'deprived'.

The theory that certain children speak a 'restricted' form of language is generally associated in the UK with the name of Basil Bernstein, though Bernstein has, since 1969, emphatically denied that he ever proposed a 'verbal deficit' theory. Bernstein's successive formulations of his position are not easy to follow. In his early papers he contrasted 'public languages' with 'formal languages' Public languages were used by working-class speakers while the middle class had access to formal languages.

A 'public language' was defined, *inter alia*, as a language of 'implicit meaning'. That is, the speaker expects his hearer to share common expectations which enable meanings to be transacted with minimal, purely linguistic signals. A perhaps simplistic example of implicit meaning might be this. Imagine a husband rises from his chair at 11.0 p.m. and goes towards the kitchen he may say 'Hm?' or 'Time?' For his wife, the monosyllable carries the implicit, quite complex,meaning: 'Shall I fill the hot-water bottle now and look up?

Formal language, by contrast, is a language of 'explicit meaning'. It relies much lesson shared expectations but explicitly spells out its meaning so as to be understood by a wider variety of hearers. The interesting hypothesis that children from certain kinds of background might be less at home in language of explicit meaning aroused widespread discussion. But even before the theory had been fully worked out, and certainly before rigorous analysis of children's language had proved the theory, Bernstein changed his ground. The notion of 'code' was substituted for 'language'. Language was defined as words actually spoken whereas a 'code' was rather a system of rules or principles, 'verbal planning activities, at the psychological level'.

At the same time the terms 'restricted' and 'elaborated' code while middle-class children can switch between these two codes, the working-class pupil has access only to the restricted code.

It should be said that it is very difficult to find in any single one of Bernstein's papers a fully worked out, integrated definition of the two codes. Nevertheless the notion that working-class pupils had access only to a restricted code caught popular attention and, whatever Bernstein's later papers said, it was with this notion that his name was linked by most teachers, and especially by those recently graduating from the college.

If Bernstein's formulations were imprecise and sometimes contradictory, it should be remembered that the field was new and knowledge was expanding rapidly. Nothing should detract from the brilliance of some of his insights in areas that had been little explored. His formulations were certainly more subtle than some of his detractors have made out or than the essays written by generations of college student might suggest.

By contrast, what has been called the 'classical verbal deficit theory', developed in the USA, was both less subtle in its formulation and easier to attack. The classical theory, which lay behind much of the Head Start programme in the USA, might be summarised as follows:

> There are two varieties of speech: a high and a low variety; the low variety lacks the necessary ingredients for learning in school;...it is the low variety that is spoken by working-class children and by most black children;...if such children are to succeed in school they must be helped to acquire the high variety as soon as possible.

After reviewing the corpus of 'classical verbal deficit' writings Gordon offers a judgement on the controversy that, he suggests, must linguists would now accept. It is worth looking at closely:

> Probably no linguist would deny that language plays a significant role in many cognitive processes-in particular, categorisation, planning, self-monitoring and abstract reasoning..What linguists do not accept are notions that any one variety of speech is intrinsically superior to another for the purpose of cognitive development. If one dialect were superior in

> cognitive terms to another, then the same would be true in an even more striking form in respect of differences between languages, and there is no evidence that speakers of any particular language are cognitively more developed by virtue of their language than speakers of any other language... any language can adopt or create new lexical items as and when conditions require.

The catch phrase here is 'cognitively more developed'. There may be two ways of thinking about the usefulness of a particular language for 'cognitive development'. The linguist may have in mind the potential capacity of any given language to serve as support for thinking or learning by providing symbols for concepts and a syntactic structure in which to manipulate the concepts. The language allows the user to define concepts precisely, to discriminate concepts that differ, to group concepts into categories, to compare them, and to form new concepts by deduction, or induction.

Now it may well be that the linguist can show that for cognition, as defined above, all languages are potentially equal. But leaving aside this quibble, and assuming that the linguist is right, the argument that all languages are potentially equal as vehicles for thinking may not help the teacher in the classroom or the pupil who wants to learn.

For there is another aspect of 'cognitive development'. This is the extent to which cognition depends on book learning: on getting access to the stored wisdom of one's community, or that of other communities. Here, as Orwell might have said, some language are decidedly more equal than others.

There is, first, the obvious distinction between those languages which have a written form and those which do not. Transmission of experience from generation to generation in a community without writing is limited by the span of human memory. If 'cognitive development' is to mean anything, the child who is limited to a language with no written form is clearly at a disadvantage compared with the speaker whose language can offer him access to books and libraries.

But there is a difference, also, between a language that can give access to *particular* ideas and knowledge and one that cannot. For example, the number of languages that can give the advanced student direct to modern linguistic theory is quite limited. Reliance on translation of ideas of great complexity must put the learner at a disadvantage.

It does not help the discussion to make untenable claims that no language can *ever* be superior to another, *for certain purposes*. What is helpful is to accept, as most socio-linguists do, that languages do *differ* greatly. The consequences of submitting the notion of difference for deficit are considerable. If we think in terms of deficit we denigrate a child's language or dialect. If we accept difference the remedy may be to change our teaching and educate ourselves to overcome linguistic prejudice and parochialism.

To put across the notion that difference can be interesting and enriching may require effort. It calls for the re-education of our community, not least of parents and teachers, in linguistic tolerance. It is a strong argument for the kind of 'awareness language' with which this book is concerned. As Gordon puts it: 'open discussion in schools of attitudes towards linguistic diversity could form a useful basis for discussion of other, equally harmful stereotyped attitudes and even of the mechanisms of stereotyping in general'.

Once we accept a 'linguistic variability hypothesis', it becomes possible to examine dispassionately the ways in which some languages may be less useful than others as learning tools in school and to consider, equally dispassionately, whether what is true of languages may also be true of dialects. It then becomes easier to discuss the real problems facing teaching in schools.

Reality of the language of education

The African writer Camara Laye has described movingly in his autobiography as brilliant boy's journey out of his tribal culture and language as he seeks an education in his native country. The tribal language into which the boy was open to him. Only through the French language could the boy qualify in the examinations that would take him to France and the higher education he sought. For his 'cognitive development' the tribal language and French were far from equal.

The same case may present itself nearer home. The London schoolboy of immigrant parents who speaks Gujerati at home cannot hope to be educated in Gujerati in London beyond the nursery level, of only because teachers, examiners and textbooks in secondary subjects are not available in his home language. No university in Britain will accept him unless he has good English and has studied his 'A' levels in English. Clearly, therefore, English and Gujerati are not merely 'different'. For practical learning purposes in London, one language is greatly 'superior' to the other. the linguistic richness, antiquity, subtlety, value as a tool for expression of thought or emotion of Gujerati are immaterial in this assessment. It is important not to muddle the two sets of considerations.

We cite these obvious cases to illustrate the way in which the linguist's humane insistence that all languages are potentially equal for cognitive development may seem in practice, to the teacher trying to help the pupils in front of him, not very helpful or meaningful.

Children of west Indian origin

A more controversial case is that of the child of West Indian origin whose home dialect is or has features of a Creole. The difficulties faced by the West Indian child in school epitomise, perhaps to an extreme degree, those faced by pupils who do not use standard English. How can the teacher best help? Peter Trudgill in an informed and sympathetic analysis distinguishes three possible approaches.

The first is to try to eliminate the non-standard speech, by preventing the child using it and correcting non-standard features as 'wrong'. Linguists, Trudgill comments, consider this approach to be mistaken psychologically and socially; but above all, they consider it mistaken because it cannot succeed.

The second approach is 'bidialectalism' and it is supported by most linguists. It accepts that non-standard forms are rightly used at home, with friends, and, in certain circumstances, in school. It treats the two varieties objectively as separate forms, both legitimate for certain purposes, and encourages 'code switching'. It requires that the teacher have some knowledge both of language teaching and of the child's dialect, and that he or she respect the child's language. This approach, Trudgill thinks, is likely to be successful only with *writing* since children will adopt the *speech* of another group only if they wish to become economically and socially accepted members of that group.

There is a third approach described by Trudgill as 'appreciation of dialect differences'. Teachers adopting this approach would teach children to *write* standard English but beyond that would try to educate opinion to accept non-standard dialects as valid systems. Trudgill admits that critics have called this approach hopelessly utopian. It would require education towards tolerance in the schools by teachers who were themselves free from linguistic prejudice: 'In the short run we may not be able to afford to abandon the bidialectalism approach'.

Part of the case for the 'awareness of language' programme for which we are arguing is that it may provide the essential background against which teachers might develop the 'bidialectalism' approach to non-standard forms of English described by Trudgill. In the long run, too, the only hope we have of achieving his ideal solution, the ultimate 'appreciation of dialect differences', is by a sustained effort at developing language awareness in the schools, in teacher training and among parents.

The challenge to teachers and teacher trainers is formidable. It is not confined to the UK. In all the great industrial democracies teachers are facing the same challenge: how to offer more equal opportunity in the school system to speakers of minority languages and non-standard dialects. The contributions of William Labov, a socio-linguist in the USA, have greatly helped to illuminate the problems. In a recent paper he reviewed a celebrated court case: the 'Black English Trial at Ann Arbor'.

The case turned on the question: What is the school called on to do when some of the pupils speak a 'non—standard' form of the language, in this case 'Black English'? The further question raised was: What exactly is the linguistic status of 'Black English'? Prior to the trial linguists were not in agreement but Labov claims that the trial concentrated their minds and they reached a consensus which was excellently expressed in the summing up of Judge Joiner:

> All of the distinguished researchers and professionals testified as to the existence of a language system, which is a part of the English language but different in significant respects from the standard English used in the school setting, the commercial world, the world of the arts and science, among the professions, and in government. It is and has been used at some time by 80 percent of the black people of this country and has as its genesis the transactional or pidgin language of the slaves, which after a generation or two became a creole language. Since then it has constantly been refined and brought closer to the mainstream of society. It still flourishes in areas where there are concentrations of black people. It contains aspects of Southern dialect and is used largely by black people in their casual conversation and informal talk.

Judge Joiner delivered his opinion on 12 July 1979. He found for the plaintiffs and directed the Ann Arbor School

Board to submit to him within thirty day a plan defining the exact steps to be taken to help. These steps would include:

(i) identifying children speaking Black English

(ii) using that knowledge in reaching such students how to read 'standard English'

Labov comments:

> In his decision, Judge Joiner expressed the view that there were no barriers to communication in the classroom. According to his observations, teachers could understand children and children could understand children. Rather, he believed that the language barrier that did exist was in the form of unconscious negative attitudes by teachers towards children who spoke Black English, and the reaction of children to those attitudes.

The plan submitted by the School Board was for in-service training for teachers that would include: twenty hours of instruction on the characteristics and history of Black English; methods for identifying speakers of the dialect; ways of distinguishing mistakes in reading from differences in pronunciation, and strategies for helping children to switch from Black English to standard English.

Labov continues:

> My own view...is that operations on attitudes alone will not be enough to make a substantial difference to the reading of black children. What is needed is a set of additions to the day-to-day reading curriculum, in order to show the teachers how to deal with students in the

> classroom who have a different linguistic system than that assumed in the curriculum. No such materials exist as yet, but some linguists have been working at putting their knowledge to use in this way.

The 'awareness of language' programme that we are advocating can claim to provide at least the essential background of knowledge and of attitudes without which the strategies for which socio-linguists like Trudgill and Labov are pleading have no chance of succeeding. Trudgill's 'bidialectalism' approach and still more his '[ideal] appreciation of dialect differences', like Labov's re-education of teachers, will only be possible as part of a sustained effort to raise standards of 'awareness of language' in schools, in training colleges and among present and future parents.

The charge of 'manipulation'

The linguist's acceptance of the need to teach at least the *written* form of standard English, for all its humane consideration of the child's learning difficulties, has, however, been condemned in some quarters. The argument, often stridently expressed, is that those who would try to teach children the standard forms are guilty of foisting on them an alien culture. Gordon considers this argument and rejects it in forthright terms. He refers to those critics who

> see traditional curricula as largely alien and meaningless to the cultural values of working-class communities [and as] the bourgeois values of the school. [What they overlook is that] all children in Britain, and their parents, live in one and the same nation state, under one and the

> same political, economic and social order... it is very much open to question how many schools are actually located in identifiable communities with clearly defined cultures of their own. In general, much of the discussion about conflict between middle-class and working-class cultures is based on very simplistic concepts of culture in a complex society.

Acceptance of linguistic differences, and the creation in school of a climate in which language difference can be discussed without prejudice, need not imply the denigration of the culture of any group, but need not carry with them any denial of the values that, in a democracy, all children should learn to share. Yet some critics would characterise even the teaching of the standard forms of English, the language of education, as 'manipulation' of pupils. The argument is mischievous and has muddled and confused many young students and teachers exposed to it on training courses.

There must be a sense, of course, in which any decision by the community to set up a school system, or to design a curriculum, indeed to teach a child anything, can be described as 'manipulating' the child. all attempts to give children the means to lead fruitful lives within the context of the community and the state of which they are citizens must be seen by the convinced anarchist, who does not believe in the state, as 'manipulation' of children. For this reason the philosophical anarchist demands that society be 'deschooled', because schools are one of the state's most powerful agencies. The doctrine of the anarchist has a long intellectual history. Within its own terms it presents a logical critique of all authority.

The believer in democracy is bound to take a very different view of the purposes of schooling. Fundamental to the theory of democracy is the concept of the 'autonomy' of the individual. Every citizen, which means every *voter,* must be presumed to be independently capable of exercising the vote. This notion of the autonomy of the individual determines the main role of the school, which is to make people as *free* as they have it in them to be.

If the purpose of education is to make individuals free, we have to ask: What are the hindrances to freedom? The 'long march' of compulsory state schooling since 1870 has been a sustained attempt to push back the threats to children's freedom. The threats include ignorance, prejudice, the sway of fashion, the lure of the market and the 'hidden persuaders' of the media. Equally limiting to freedom, of course, is a lack of the skills needed to survive in the environment, such as the means to earn a living: or, more basically, lack of the sheer knowledge needed to understand what is happening in one's community.

If the democrat is asked: what are schools for? he must answer that at their best they must be *refuges* within which freedom from outside pressures can be guaranteed and within which the *apprenticeship in autonomy,* which is vital for a democracy, can be learned. Those who plan the curriculum have a heavy responsibility and the best of them will never lose sight of the main objective which must be to help children to learn how to exercise freedom.

It is against this concept of the school that proposals for the reform of language education should be judged. Those who oppose the reform on the grounds that teaching 'language' is 'manipulation' of children must be challenged to answer two questions. First, are they arguing that the whole curriculum is 'manipulation' and therefore that schooling itself stands condemned? And, second, why, having had the good fortune themselves to acquire the language of education, do they feel justified in arguing that the same opportunity to learn should be denied to the children now in school?

Failure to master the mother tongue

We have perhaps said enough to justify giving greater attention to fostering the right attitudes to language among pupils, teachers and especially parents, who are often the most linguistically prejudiced.

This in itself would make a strong case for the kind of 'awareness of language' courses whose development in schools we have traced earlier.

By bringing round the table, in the planning stage, teachers of English, of foreign languages and of ethnic mother tongues, and speakers of Creole, they have begun a dialogue 'across the *language* curriculum' that has not hitherto taken place in schools.

Discussion in such boards of language studies may help to put into perspective two aspects of language learning which some recently fashionable views in linguistics have confused rather than clarified. The issues can be put in the form of questions:

(a) At what age can normal children be assumed to have 'learned' their mother tongue?

(b) Do all children reach a comparable level of competence in their mother tongue or are there some children whose competence is markedly different from the norm?

One recently influential school of linguistics in effect answers both questions quite dogmatically. Thus, in Noam Chomsky's words, towards the end of his famous excoriating review of B.F. Skinner's *Verbal Behaviour:*

> this task [learning the mother tongue] is accomplished in an astonishingly short time, to a large extent independently of intelligence, and in a comparable way by all children.. Any theory of learning must cope with these facts ...all normal children acquire essentially comparable grammars of great complexity with remarkable rapidity.

If we are to take this to mean anything more than that all speakers of English learn comparable versions of the grammar of English, that is, if it means that all speakers learn the grammar to comparable stages of *mastery,* then the claim is seriously misleading to teachers. Yet many linguists follow Chomsky in assuming that the child's acquisition of syntax is virtually complete by the age of 5.

It was this assumption that Carol Chomsky set out to investigate in a famous study which prompted many subsequent studies. She followed the progress of a group of forty children aged between 5 and 10, testing their ability to understand sentences of the form: 'John is easy to understand' and 'complement constructions' with verbs: 'see', 'promise' and 'tell'. She found that some pupils had not mastered these constructions by the age of 9 and one was still unsure of the form 'John asked Bill what to do', at the age of 10.

Other investigators have questioned the general application of some of Carol Chomsky's conclusions but in the light of her study it is difficult to maintain the assumption that the acquisition of syntax is complete by the end of the pre-school stage. It is an assumption that would find little support from practising teachers, accustomed to correcting the written work of adolescents, or even of university students!

Nor does the notion find support from psychology. Research on children's memory shows that clear notions of time are slow to develop. Without them it is not clear how a child can be said to operate the tense system within the syntax of English. I.M.L. Hunter, Professor of Psychology at the University of Keele, describes children's notion of time in these terms:

> The observations of Stern and others suggest that the performance of recalling is not achieved until early in the second year of life and does not appear with any great frequency until around the age of three. But even when experiences are recalled, there is little question of their being referred to any definite point of past time, *for the simple reason that the child has yet to develop a clear notion of time*. Even the 4-year-old has little more than an indefinite notion of 'long ago' and a broad distinction between 'earlier' and 'later' He cannot refer an event to 'the day before yesterday' or to 'last week' with any probability of accuracy.. Sometimes he can accurately locate a recalled experience as having happened 'today' or 'not today', but he can scarcely use 'yesterday' as a more exact location for experiences from the less immediate past. So far as he is capable of making temporal distinctions between his recollected experiences, he does so by reference to places: 'That was at so-and-so's house', or 'That was at such-and-

> such a town' ...he simply seems to place one event in the context of a more outstanding event without any clear reference to its location in a temporal order of events... and it is not until after the age of six years that he acquires an awareness of his own past as a historical sequence of events.

Any description of the kind of syntax acquired before the age of 6 must take account of Professor Hunter's evidence concerning the absence of a notion of time.

If language acquisition must be seen as a long-term process what of our other question: Do all children reach a 'comparable competence' or progress at comparable speed? The evidence is that they do not and that this is due partly to inmate and partly to environmental factors.

First, as to innate capacity, the precocity of girls in acquiring language is well attested. With any of the accepted tests, the evidence shows that girls, on average, begin to outstrip boys from the age of 2. By the age of 11, girls' verbal competence is so far ahead of that of boys that special measures were always taken, in the days when boys and girls took a common selection examination for places in the selective 'grammar' schools, to scale up the marks of boys in English tests, in order not to allocate a disproportionate number of girls to the scarce selective places.

The superior verbal aptitude of girls was confirmed in an interesting study by the National Foundation for Educational Research. For the purpose of their evaluation of French in the primary school the NFER team tested large cohorts of children not only in French but *inter alia,* in English comprehension and in certain aspects of formal

English grammar. The girls at age 11 scored consistently higher than the boys in all the tests of English.

The consistent superiority of girls over boys when tested for *production* of language is also demonstrated, though to a less marked degree, in scores for *reading.* In the series of measurements of national reading scores carried out by the NFER for the Department of Education between 1948 and 1971, girls scored consistently higher than boys, the difference generally reaching the 'significant' level. The results are summarised in *The Trend of Reading Standards* by K. B. Start and B.K. Wells.

In this connection the anthropologist Gordon W. Hewes in *Language Origins,* 1973, p. 115 comments:

> No one seriously supposes that the consistent precocity of girls in acquiring speech and their lower incidence of speech defects can be attributed to cultural learning differences.. The point is that are compatible with our reconstruction of early hominid behaviour, in which males would have been the principal hunters, trackers and protectors of the group-with a survival premium on ability to analyse environmental noises as well as spatial and constructional abilities-whereas females, as the main transmitters of speech to infants as well as the sex with the greater need to detect the emotional overtones of vocal messages, could be expected to be more precocious in language learning and less prone to speech defects.

Bolinger, in the same study, cities the fact that females are almost never dyslexic as suggesting that they have a more stable genetic equipment for language.

If there are clear indications that aptitude for language learning, both of the mother tongue and of foreign languages, may be partly innate, it is equally clear that aptitude is also strongly affected by the environment. the NFER study referred to above, which confirmed the superiority of girls at both French and English, also found a linear correlation between test scores in English and *parental occupation.* This merely confirmed the findings of a long series of studies which show conclusively that home background correlates closely with test score in both spoken and written language.

One obvious environmental variables is *extent* of reading. One of the more interesting off-shoots of the research by Carol Chomsky referred to earlier was her finding that the rate at which her subjects mastered the rules of syntax correlated closely with the amount of reading that each one did at home. It is not only to young children that this applies. Very much of the imagery and metaphor which is the common currency of our language was coined first and set in circulation over the centuries by great writers. Speakers of the language differ greatly in their mastery of this linguistic inheritance. It is only by thoughtful reading that competence in this area of usage can be won. The reader whose experience is limited to writing that is of little insight and reliant on borrowed cliche will simply be less competent in the use of the language at its most effective than the reader more familiar with the linguistic inheritance.

It does no service to children to pretend that, though in every other cognitive area there is along apprenticeship to be served, somehow, in language learning, the rules are different and there is no need for apprenticeship, no difference between the precision and integrity of some language, and language that is slipshod and imitative. As in other areas of learning, genetic and environmental factors may work together so subtly that it is impossible to disentangle them. However it may be explained, the fact is that by the time they reach the age of 5 children differ widely in their acquisition of their mother tongue. Yet, curiously, the extent to which speakers of any given dialect, whether it be London Jamaican or 'received standard', may differ in their competence *in their home dialect* has had little place in the discussions of socio-linguists.

In order to talk about 'language' as an abstract concept it has been convenient to pre-suppose an 'ideal speaker/hearer', equipped with something called 'adult mastery' of the language. Teachers, faced with flesh and blood pupils exchanging acts of speech are daily reminded that all individuals do not enjoy an equal competence. The picture of the speech community that the teacher sees is one of long road along which the speakers are strung out, as they advance at very different speeds, towards a goal of an ideal competence *which none will ever reach.* The linguistic distance along this road separating the front runners from those who trail behind, limping and breathless, is immense.

Once we substitute this real picture for the linguist's abstraction we are compelled to rethink two related issues which some linguists have declared closed. They are:

(a) The debate about the meaning of 'correct/incorrect' language use.

(b) The need to reformulate the discussion of 'language deficit', using the term not in the 'classical' sense of the deficiency of certain 'codes' or dialects *in themselves,* but in the new sense that some, possibly many, speakers travel less far along the road into the usage and awareness *of their dialect* than others.

'Language is what is ay, not what you say I ought to say'

It is an axiom in linguistics that 'language is what people say, not what some people think they ought to say'. There is an obvious sense in which this must be true. The linguist takes as his raw material current usage of the language. But it does not follow that all speakers to whom the linguist listens are *using* the language with equal authority. Each individual's usage has to be learned over a long period, even over a lifetime. Many speakers never cease improving mastery of their own language. Also one speaker's usage will be more 'authoritative' than another's in the sense that the speaker has mastered more completely the usage of his/her own speech community.

We can see this clearly if we consider one, admittedly narrow area, namely, mastery of vocabulary. In a discipline such as physics, language usage has developed in step with the discoveries of the laws of the discipline itself. Learning physics therefore is, in large part, learning the 'correct' matching of concepts to linguistic symbols. Matching is 'correct' when those who have made the discoveries and done the experiments to prove the concepts are in agreement. It is the discipline of physics that has established the 'correct' matching of language to such concepts as 'mass', 'latent heat' and 'gravitation', which the aspiring physicist is not at liberty to vary. The aspiring physicist's usage of language is thus less *authoritative* that of his tutor, *within that discipline.*

But it is the same story wherever we look at language in use. The student learning the law seeks to learn the 'correct' usage of words such as 'evidence',. The young musician is not free to vary the usage of the vocabulary of music. If the medical student hopes to qualify as a doctor he would be wise not to call the 'femur' the 'tibia' in front of his professor, nor the budding cook decide that 'grilling' and 'frying' are interchangeable terms. Of course the 'front runners' are busy creating new language as the discipline advances. But, even for them, in every other area of language usage there is a long apprenticeship to be served.

Each individual's use of language will reflect how far his particular apprenticeship has taken him. But the speaker who is more competent can say, not simply what concept a given word does evoke for him but also, within the areas of the language which he has truly mastered, what concept the word *ought* to evoke. His authority for the 'ought' is simply greater acquaintance with usage in that particular area.

Degrees of competence

There is, then, a valid distinction, which has been blurred by some recent discussions, between what people say and what they would say if they were more informed. Competence and 'intuition of the native speaker' may be useful concepts in linguistics, so long as it is remembered that they are relative terms.

If we were discussing the competence of English-speaking pupils in, say, French, German or Spanish, the point would scarcely be worth making. The pupil just beginning the foreign language does not use it with the same authority as his teacher. He cannot claim that 'French is what I say'. Yet it may not be very different in the mother tongue classroom. Of course linguists will always be interested in language 'as she is spoke'. But they must remember that many of the speakers to whom they listen will still be learning the language, whatever their age.

The researcher in child language distinguishes a series of steps along the road to 'adult' language use. What is often overlooked is that the road does not suddenly end at an arbitrary point. Language acquisition is a life-long apprenticeship. Much of secondary education and of university study is a matter of extending competence in the mother tongue in defined areas, matching, with increasing discrimination, new language, or old language used in more precise ways, to new concepts of great complexity.

This gives a different gloss to loosely used phrases such as 'verbal deficit.' The debate about 'restricted' varieties is seen to have been peripheral and unhelpful. It is not a question of certain dialects or codes being 'disadvantaged' in themselves, nor of implied comment on any social or racial groups. We are concerned, as teachers, with individual children, whatever their dialect. The crucial difference between some of our pupils and others is that some achieve a greater competence than others in *their own dialect.*

Language and thought

To argue that individuals differ in important ways in their linguistic competence and in their intuitions concerning the language usage of their own group is not to suppose any simple causal relationship between language mastery and cognition. The question of the link between language and learning is complex and controversial. In the course of his apprenticeship in the language usage of his community the learner's progress in the language must, to a great extent, *depend* on his cognition. In the early stages especially language 'waits upon cognition'. Equally, language learning may later take the lead and make possible certain cognitive steps that would otherwise be impossible. As the school process develops language increasingly leads in the interplay with cognition. Crucial ways in which the language of school seems to take the lead and facilitate cognition are:

(i) 'signposting' concepts not yet met, pointing to the fact that they exist and should be explored, much as a signpost shows that the road leads to a town not yet reached;

(ii) allowing concepts to be stored in the filing cabinet of the memory in such a way that they can be retrieved economically;

(iii) using language to control one's own behaviour, a phenomenon observed in young children but more common in adults. Consider the example, quoted by Cook, of the aircraft pilot running through a verbal checklist of precautions before take off;

(iv) enabling the speaker/hearer to be emancipated from the here and now and to think of, and refer to, events distant in time and space.

In sum, language makes possible the process of 'categorisation': that is the arrangement of concepts in 'sets' or 'categories' which belong together. As suggested above, in the earliest stages the process that take the lead is cognition, that is the child's recognition of the 'categories' of concepts into which the initially haphazard sense impressions received from the chaotic universe fall. As the child grows older it is language that increasingly takes the lead and makes possible the complex categorisation which Bruner called 'the calculus of thought'

It is significant that all these processes become increasingly essential as the exploration of the school disciplines unfolds. Whether the child is learning to solve problems in geometry, or to distinguish 'mixtures' from 'compounds' in chemistry, the 'categories' which the language allows the child to distinguish and compare become the building blocks of future learning. The quality of the learning - the strength of the building - will depend on the clarity with which one conceptual 'set' is distinguished from the other, the sharpness of their outlines, and the speed and dexterity with which they are handled. This depends on precision in matching concepts to language.

Can 'awareness' affect 'competence'?

The advocate of giving an important role to 'awareness of language' has a further question to answer, however. Granted that language provides the building blocks of school learning, is it the case that deepening pupils' *awareness* will lead to great *competence*? Are the two causally linked?

Professor Halliday and his colleagues, in the Introduction to *Language in Use,* answer the question in this way:

> there is...a crucial relationship between the two. The long argument over the teaching of 'grammer' in schools really concentrated upon the effects of a certain kind of explicit knowledge of the language, such as classification of words and parsing, on pupils' use of language. When teachers discovered that there

> seemed to be no observable effect of the one of the other, they rejected teaching about language, because they could see no justification for it. It was unfortunate that the study of language came to be identified with a rudimentary and inadequate type of knowledge about language, and that its validity was judged solely upon its power to increase competence.

Language in use offers a form of language study which can be valued as a rewarding end in itself, namely the development of awareness. However, a basic premise of the volume is that *the development of awareness in the pupil will have a positive effect on his competence,* though this effect is likely to be indirect and may not show up immediately. A second premise is that what is well-rehearsed through being talked out in discussion, especially where the discussion involves groups of three to five, will have a similar oblique, delayed but quite positive effective upon pupils' command of the written language.

Whatever their potential, pupils often find themselves unable to handle the language which the processes of explicit analysis and impersonal comment require, and it is the use of language of this kind that makes up so large a part of the working lives of most pupils. The development of awareness has a marked effect upon a pupil's ability to cope with the whole range of his work, because he comes to see that many problems are not so much problems in grasping the content of what he studies, but problems in handling the language appropriate to it.

The reference in this passage to the effect of discussion in small groups on acquisition of the *written* language is extremely interesting:

> the preparation for reading should include, as a most important component, attempts to make children more aware of the spoken tongue. It is not just a matter of helping them to use speech more effectively, it is a matter of helping them to notice what they are doing.

In an earlier passage Donaldson reminds us how difficult the breakthrough to reading is for some pupils:

> As literate adults, we have become so accustomed to the written word that we seldom stop to think how dramatically it differs from spoken one. The spoken word...exists for a brief moment as one element in a tangle of shifting events - from which it must be disentangled if it is to be separately considered - and then fades. The written word endures... We may return to it tomorrow. By its very nature it can be quite free of non-linguistic context. So the child's first encounters with books provide him with much more favourable opportunities for *becoming aware* of language in its own right than his earlier encounters with the spoken word are likely to have done.

Short term memory

A point that is implicit in what Donaldson says, but which is not developed in her argument, is that learning to read sets the learner free from the severe restraints of the Short Term Memory. Processing of the spoken message is entirely dependent on being able to hold it in the STM for long enough to identify its components and recognise the pattern(s) which determine the meaning. The listener cannot control the speed at which the message arrives an must process the components strictly in the order in which they arrive. By contrast the components of the written message can be scanned repeatedly *and in any order.* Research on the rapid eye movements made by practised readers as the text is scanned show how important this facility is.

It is this that explains one great difference between listening and reading, namely the *speed* with which messages can be taken in. Mattingley estimates that the maximum speed for reading with meaning is 2,000 wpm against a mere 400 for listening. The breakthrough to reading clearly means a change of gear in learning.

It is relevant to remember that the capacity of the STM has, since the early days of IQ tests, been known to be systematically related both to age and to IQ measures. Testing the number of digit that could be retained in the STM was one of the devices used in early intelligence tests such as the Stanford-Binet and the Wechsler batteries. The STM span increases on the Stanford-Binet scale from two digits at age 30 months, to three digits at 36 months, and four at 54 months and stabilises in adulthood at about seven digits.

However it has been demonstrated that there is no systematic relationship between STM span and language learning. To explain this Olson goes back to an observation by Miller that STM capacity can be increased by imposing *pattern* on the incoming message. This ability to impose pattern is *learned:* 'The performance deficits we find in younger children's remembering are due to failure to organise, plan, monitor and integrate their information processing'. It is not that children cannot process incoming messages so that they retain more of them in the

STM: 'children as young as 3 or 4, if not younger, can employ many of the strategies they will later use routinely in remembering. But unless prompted they do not'. Olson concludes: 'language presents the earliest and most acute challenge to the child's ability to handle information in real time'. The irony is that though the mastery of reading sets the child free from the restraints of the STM on processing messages, yet the breakthrough itself comes only *after* the processing strategies have reached a certain level.

This brings us back to the need for one-to-one dialogue with an adult and the need for 'adult time' in the home, in order to allow the processing strategies to be practised, upon which, in due course, the reading skill can be built.

To sum up: much recent discussion of the relationship of language and learning, like the debate about 'verbal deficit', has seemed to assume that language learning is a single, all-or-nothing, process. It has overlooked the fact that acquiring the mother tongue is a process in two distinct stages. The second stage, mastery of the written language, seems to depend on a high degree of 'awareness' of, and hence the ability to 'process', the spoken form.

Far more children than is commonly imagined never achieve the degree of awareness that is called for and so never master written language with confidence and relish.

2

Language and Higher Education

The crisis in higher education in India is seen by many as resulting from a system rooted in the colonial past. Edward Shills goes to the extent of saying that 'India' is not an intellectually independent country but it is still intellectually a province of the British metropolis. The past is very often used as a scapegoat for present lapses in India, but in all fairness to the British system it must be said that, if at all India is intellectually a province of the British metropolis, it reflects the metropolis of the late eighteenth and nineteenth centuries, and not of the twentieth.

For education has bypassed the majority of people in India. It has ceased to be a storehouse of tradition and a generator of values consistent with the composite culture of India and appropriate to its state of development—economic, political and cultural.

Many educationists and statesmen consider innovations and change in the pattern of education essential for social change in India. Labels like job-oriented education, vocational education, work experience in education, etc.. are created to give a new look to the old structure. In this chapter an attempt will be made to raise some fundamental issues, to analyse the causes of chaos and confusion, and examine the relevance of courses of study with regard to the emergent social realities in the country.

The Indian academic system is monolithic in character. All universities, by and large, follow one uniform practice, be it admissions, appointments to faculties, the framing of syllabi or examinations. Since the appointment of the first Education Commission, each Commission has said essentially the same thing about all the important matters relating to education. However, after each report so much energy is spent on the fringes of the problem and so many surface adjustments and compromises are made that at the most the system could be termed 'Ordered Imperfection.' It is seldom realized that it is impossible to build an efficient system from inefficient components. By propping up education as it was, enriching an outmoded system and building redundancy into it a progressive increase of internal conflict has occurred and the entire system is condemned to failure.

Good examples of this chaos and redundancy are provided by decision makers in regard to syllabus and curriculum. It is a common belief even among educationists that a mere increase in the number of years of instruction will raise the standard of attainment in a subject. This is why without an adequate input in teacher training, improved instructional material and the use of up-to-date instructional technology, demands were made in may parts of the country to introduce instruction in

English in the lower classes. An example of a different kind of redundancy is provided by the subject specialists. In order to strengthen science and technology, specialists are often invited to examine syllabi of various science subjects. Such experts in consultation with their colleagues in India prepare syllabi in their respective subjects, which may be ideal if those particular topics were taught, but do not quite fit into the general Indian framework either in terms of allocation of emphasis or in terms of balancing of content. Schooling is equated with the composite of the objectives set for subjects and the process as well as the product of teaching is lost sight of.

The curricula of universities continue today with utter disregard for the many changes and innovations that have taken place in the field of education and in the use of educational technology. Even the teaching of the dominant language of the area as mother tongue follows the age old pattern. This has little to offer by war of challenge either to the present or provide a strategy to build for the future. Because of this prevalent confusion even the dominant languages are not sufficiently developed to cope with the demands made on them and as a result the foundation of education grows weaker day by day.

With the attainment of independence by India there was a natural urge among the people of the country to enjoy the full rights and benefits of citizenship. Unfortunately in spite of all the talk of socialism and equality, there continues to be a minority elite and consequently the large majority of the people suffer from a disadvantage. Big cities with a higher population attract a larger number of colleges, thus ensuring higher education for the more affluent and advanced sections of society. In the state of Uttar Pradesh, 22 cities with a population of two lakhs and above 32% of all the colleges in the state. The survey conducted by the National Council of Educational Research and Training on the sociology of education reveals that 80% of the university entrants and graduates come from the top 20% of Society. The poverty sector is barred from this education. On the other hand, whether it is the basic education or the mother tongue education, all so-called educational experiments have been made at the cost of the under-privileged. Indian education, instead of being geared to the need of the disadvantaged, has put emphasis on the perpetuation of the elite minority and bestowed rank, status and wealth on those who worship it. A curious contradiction has been built up in the process. On the one hand, there is a persistent demand for more of the same kind of education even if it leads to unemployment, and on the other, there is an equally persistent demand to destroy and scrap the system as it is purposeless and ineffective.

The rising expectations and aspirations of the majority of the people, consequent on the attainment of independence, were never reflected in the courses of study in the academic institutions. In structure, content and orientation they remain almost unchanged. Educationists have been satisfied with a mere enumeration of class hours, and at best major ideas and concepts, without being bothered about their relevance either to their times or to the present. Not to speak of modernity, it appears that not even contemporaneity was, nor is a major concern of the educationists. Without a detailed critical examination of all the courses of study in history, on the basis of a cursory overview it can be safely stated that Indian history after 1945 and Indian regional history after 1885 has almost no place in the history curriculum. What is much more alarming is that in many universities the preoccupation is still British history and what passes in the name of Indian history is a extension of the colonial history in an Indian locale. When ancient Indian history and culture is considered to be of antiquarian interest and thus of interest to only antiquarians and modern Indian history is considered inconsequential, it is futile to look either for historicity in a national context or a sense of historical perspective among the youth of the day.

Both the structure and the function of the academic system in the country inhibit the pursuit of excellence. Pursuit of excellence pre-suppose an atmosphere of academic freedom, simulation and initiative. With the attainment of freedom from alien rule, although freedom from a number of restraints was achieved, in the academic sphere this 'freedom from' was never translated into 'freedom of.' The elitists minority enjoyed a few licences because of limited access to education, but neither the student community as a whole nor the people at large got a chance to taste liberty, particularly the liberty to choose and to refashion on archaic reality. The system offered very little variation in approach, or courses of study in specific goal oriented training to permit genuine choice.

The infrastructure of the constituent institutions within the system being pyramidal and the sole criterion of upward movement being seniority, there is little scope for competition for excellence even among the faculty. Whatever little scope exists is easily stifled by the seniors who are at the apex of the 'downward flowing system of decision making.' When reward is consequent upon seniority, excellence can be a positive disadvantage. The seniors, who were at one time extremely competent, have no way of coping with the explosion of knowledge and thus very soon become outdated in their respective disciplines. Any new knowledge is considered a threat to their charisma as Head, and an affront to their limited capability and absolute authority. In their effort to retain their privileges, the 'Heads' discourage genuine competition. Thus, the entire system is immunized to adaptation and innovation.

The machinery which was set up to coordinate activities, determine standards and give grants-in-aid to institutions of higher education has never in the past effectively used it powers. As a result limits of central corrective action in professionalizing education were never establish. To illustrate, instead of emphasizing on its professional character, and providing intrinsically academic leader-ship, the University Grants Commission, with Vice-Chancellors participating as decision markers, acted as an apex institution distributing patronage. Both participating and retired seniors continued an obsolescent debate. This neither took note of the search for a new set of operational paradigms among the newly trained academics nor of the depth of the ferment among the youth in a hurry to telescope the process of discovery and innovation, attain modernity and acquire new and contemporary knowledge. There is certainly an incipient conflict even within this new set of goals and their articulation with a policy is a complex enterprise. But the point is that decision-making hardly matched the tasks facing it .

Universities have become degree-granting bodies. In 1973 about seven lakh students took their Bachelors and Masters Degrees in Arts. Science and Commerce. The number has considerably increased since then. The degree holders are service-oriented rather than job-oriented. It is common knowledge that an average agriculture graduate has a lesser grasp of realities than an average illiterate farmer in his field. The same is true of almost all vocational subjects with probably a difference in degree. In most cases there is a disproportionate emphasis on teaching about a vocation rather than on teaching the vocation itself. As ar result persons trained vocationally often lack the self-confidence to start an independent project where they have to compete and establish their superior talent over other competitors.

In a transitional society struggling to change from tradition to modernity, emphasis needs to be put on the encouragement of giftedness and creativity. This is necessary for breaking the stagnation and inertia inherent in the traditional mode of thinking. Since an infinitesimally small percentage of people participating in the benefits of education is called upon to provide leadership in thought and action, unless this class is creative and gifted, the country is bound to slip into mediocrity. However, when custodians of past knowledge are in the apex positions in education guarding their positions of privilege, it is futile to expect them to encourage giftedness and creativity.

The mode of syllabus-making also inhibits creativity. The syllabus is mode two, three or four years before an examination is held. The process of changing the syllabus is consequently slow. To that extent syllabuses are out of tune with contemporary knowledge. Added to that the time gap existing between the creation of new knowledge at different centres of the world and their availability to our system, the tendency in the system is to conform to 'inherited fixed concepts and practices.' In the absence of a built-in guarantee for continuing training of academics, the system, instead of encouraging a spirit of exploration, follow the path of least resistance and promotes conformism. This comes into instant conflict with the youth's immense capacity for enquiry and his yearning for change. The present chaos is an expression of this strain.

Changing educational strategies assume shifting academic objectives in the light of emergent social realities in the context of change. Unfortunately no professional mechanism exists either to define the goals from time to time or examine the suitability of the available instructional apparatus. In the State Secretariat where Indian Administrative Service Officers are considered omniscient, very little fundamental thinking in this regard can be expected. Similar results obtain from the multiplicity of controls and agencies within the government bureaucracy and from the well-known ineffectuality of Vice-Chancellors with their less than perfect credentials for academic leadership.

The effort of the academic leaders in India has been concentrated on rehabilitating the product rather than rectifying the system. For instance, degrees continue to be multiplied and decried at the same breath, and then programmes of rehabilitation of the degree owners are undertaken. Higher positions in the faculty are created, but the products of the seniority system are promoted to them. Very little action is taken to relate professional status to professional performance. The subject content is improved, a good curriculum is prepared and yet at the same time education is made solely dependent on the text book. Because of well-intentioned measures corrective schools are started, more resources added, more trained personnel and improved physical facilities created; but all these have the effect of adding layers to the existing system and do not add up to a wide-ranged vision for the education of tomorrow.

It is important to recognize that the drop-outs and failures at different levels of education, the mounting educated unemployment, the reported mass-copying, factionalism among the faculty and the destruction of academic institutions are symptoms of a deeper malady. They signal the rejection of the system by various segments connected with it. Unless efforts are made to radically rectify it to ensure a two-way flow of decision making and to relate education to the needs of the community, the system will collapse under its own weight.

Language is an important factor in linking education with society. The language debate in India has mixed up the two questions of language instruction and language as a medium of instruction. Most of the contemporary debates on this question also err on the confusion of language as a medium of instruction with the content of instruction. It is not realized that no matter what the language of instruction, the contemporaneity of the scientific books is in inverse ratio to the active work done in these fields. The obsolescence of these books are directly related to the obsolescence of theories, ideas or even facts in these fields.

In a Dutch High School the students on one occasion pointed out to their excellent biology teacher teaching the difficult subject of genetics, that 'what he told them was in conflict with the textbook'. He then sternly peered over his glasses and announced emphatically, 'I am the book'. In India, where the mastery of the textbook is considered the goal of instruction, it is no wonder that there is more concern about translating textbooks than about exciting the sense of adventure and exploration of the young students as a passport to the world of knowledge. Prof. Satyen Bose, a scientist of the Bose-Einstein statistics fame, one commented that if someone cannot impart an intricate problem of his field to his audience in his mother tongue, it is not because he does not know his mother tongue, but because he does not know his subject. After two hundred years of repetition of other people's views, the system has begun to develop a rootless pseudo-internationalism where restricted textbook knowledge is imparted through a foreign language. No wonder that a foreign textbook enjoys greater status. This inhibits original thinking and as out of school mother tongue is devalued and derided, leads people to learn their mother tongues in schools.

It is generally accepted, on sound pedagogical grounds, that the mother tongue is best suited as the medium of instruction. It is the natural language of thought for the child and eminently suited for concept formation. While any language may be the language of added comprehension, only the language with which one lives and grows is best in achieving originality in thought and expression. If a language has not been exploited for expressing certain abstruse concepts, it is due to no inherent defect in that language. Language can only be enriched through use, and so the argument that a language cannot be used because it is not rich is putting the horse before the cart.

A lot of fruitless debate is going on due to the confusion between the percolation of knowledge and sharing of knowledge. The percolation of knowledge to the popular level or the spread of knowledge among the masses is essential for raising the general standard of education. But it must be recognized that underlying this is an attitude of condescension. It ignores the fact that without the benefit of accumulated knowledge and wisdom at the folk level knowledge created at the top could be sterile and irrelevant. It is important to strengthen the foundation of a reservoir of knowledge which could be shared with the large majority of people in the country who are discriminated against by formal education. This must be differentiated from the sharing of knowledge among the intellectual elites not only within the country, but also outside the country. It is clear that opportunities must be created for the educated people of the country to communicate with the peers in any part of the world as well as with the seekers of knowledge in any part of the country. For that purpose provision must be made to offer as many language courses to suit as many specific needs as possible. Realistically in India such provision must begin with English and Hindi. But because of a lack of clear national perspective on the part of enthusiasts in both the camps, the quality of education has not improved.

Today in India, between the provincial and the extra-territorial intellectual allegiance of the anglophiles, whether it is to England or to New York, the concept of country is lost. On the other hand, between the narrow parochial self-seeking and the avarice for power of the Hindi fanatics, the concept of country is equally blurred. When looked through either looking glass, there will be no country left to be emotionally integrated. The existence of such a state of affairs is exemplified by the threats and counter threats of ultimatum and secession by various extremist positions. Such threats have very little academic relevance. Higher education has suffered most as it has not been able to extricate itself from the self-defeating arguments of both the camps.

English education in India has resulted in adding one more national language to the already existing fifteen. It has also resulted in the decline of multi-lingualism. By encouraging attitudes ranging from indifference to positive disrespect towards the traditional Indian languages, English education has also generated a good deal of mutual disrespect among them. As in Switzerland, such a situation poses a threat to the unity of the country.

Various formulae have been suggested from time to time to meet this situation. The word 'formula', like talisman and magic cure, has an unfortunate connotation of effortless problem-solving. It either invokes the meaning of a prescription and injects a sense of compulsiveness, or is adjudged the result of compromise and induces groups to demand further concessions. In either case, it helps both those who interpret formula as a way of escape from reality and those who act in defence of the existing order. The inadequacy of 'formulae' is also evident from the outward allegiance and inward betrayal.

The demand for Indian languages to be the medium of education can be traced to the early 19th century. The Bombay Education Society expressed itself in favour of the native language as the medium of instruction as far back as 1821. Ever since independence, time limits for a change-over in the instruction media have been set by the Centre as well as by individual universities. Bombay University in 1959 had set a time-limit of ten years beginning from 1960 to switch-over to the medium of Hindi. Gujarat University had imposed on itself a similar time-limit to switch to the regional language medium.

While everybody paid lip service to this principle, very little was done to move towards this end. On the contrary, the protagonists sent their wards to the English schools and conducted the vernacular experiment at the cost of others' children. The gulf in precept and practice on the part of the academic and political leadership has created not only frustration, but also bitterness among the people in general.

Nationalism in the sense of pride of national identity, as opposed to chauvinism and national insularity, is missing in the current language debate in India. As Ralph Bunche put it aptly in an international congress of educationists in the US, there has been an 'appalling loss and lack of integrity in position, in intellect, in utterance' among the politicians, administrators, and academicians discussing the issue. This is as much true of the USA as of India. As the governmental leaders have not correctly delineated the rightful place of Hindi and English, shrewd political leaders have taken advantage of the situation and confused the issue to their advantage by asking if we were getting '14 languages in exchange of English'. In the early 19th century, when language poets were eulogizing their respective mother tongues and politicians were firmly rooted in their regions, there was much more national cohesiveness and pride than there is to be seen at present.

English poses an artificial barrier against the massive 'revolution of rising expectations' of the people in gaining their rightful place in the governmental process. If the clamour of the large uneducated masses for swiftly reaping the benefits of industrialization is to be canalized in a constructive way to buy time to save democracy, they must be given an education which guarantees them a sense of belonging. of continuity, and of onward progress. This sense can only be imparted through the mother tongue, the culture language, or one of the related languages. Those who demand the maintenance of the status-quo or a go-slow policy are advocates of a static solution for a dynamic situation, and are oblivious of the fact that forces of change are 'fiercely, drivingly, unpredictably at work'.

The translation of textbooks is often cited as an insurmountable barrier in any change-over from one medium to another. The Indian academic mind is so conditioned to accepting the textbook as the master in the classroom and textbook-teaching as the goal of instruction, that both the governmental agencies and the universities can not see beyond it. In this age of explosion of knowledge, the contemporaneity of textbooks in any language is short-lived. Any original research done in French, German, Russian, Japanese is translated into English, and, to that extent, there is an information time-lag between English and those languages. That is why a study of foreign languages is considered a must for those opting for higher education in the English-speaking countries. Under the circumstances, those who are arguing in good faith in favour of translating all textbooks for all times to come are arguing in defence of mediocrity without their being aware of it.

Some centuries back when the Greek historian Herodotus decided to travel throughout the world before he wrote the history of his own people, he visited Egypt which was famous for its prowess and knowledge. He asked the omniscient priests of Egypt the cause of the flood in the river Nile. The custodians of the static knowledge in Egypt, who had never bothered to worry themselves about such causes, looked at Herodotus with consternation and pity. They are reported to have blurted out, 'Oh you Greeks, will you always remain children?' When knowledge is confined to textbooks in archives, any further quest for new knowledge is naturally considered uncomfortable or even embarrassing by the traditional authorities. Although such situations have arisen in ancient Greece, Egypt, and India, people hardly seem to have learnt any lessons from them.

Books are written in any language to put newly discovered facts, newly propounded theories or newly thought ideas before a wider public. Depending on the amount of original work done in any field of study, new facts are discovered, new inventions made. Old theories are discarded with a rapidity which makes books obsolete even before they have a chance to reach their audience. The aim of education should be to excite the sense of adventure and exploration of the students to enable them to create, invent and discover rather than trail behind other people's discoveries and inventions.

Because of the very nature of the structure of Indian education, Indian educational institutions inhibit the inculcation and diffusion of new knowledge. In a non-competitive seniority system, there is hardly any incentive for creativity on the part of the faculty. In following a rigid curriculum, the academicians seem to have come to the conclusion that the goal of instruction is teaching one or more textbooks. This is why in the current language debate, some academicians have argued in favour of English so that we may be able to import text books from England and America. There is no denying that it is imperative for our students to study books written in English. But instead of talking of books or reference books, I see no reason why so much stress should be placed on text books. I am reminded of a boy who wanted to send a telegram to his father, saying that his brother had passed a certain examination. 'Brother passed', as a statement, was too bland for him and so to make it more elegant he added the word 'away'. To those of our academicians who talk only in terms of textbooks, the word 'books' is perhaps too bland.

Textbooks in india ar neither supporting instruments of learning nor are they the base around which instruction is planned. As people who worship images as a step to the abstract and infinite remain bound to the image and seldom transcend it, those who are tutored with textbooks remain chained to it. They seldom graduate to books.

Studying a single textbook in any course is considered a very poor performance almost all the world over. Collateral reading broadens the vista of the student, helps him grasp the issues involved by presenting different points of view. Even prescription of more than one textbook is no substitute for studying a broad range of books. Any translation programme may select a number of standard up-to-date books some of which may be used as reference books in courses of study. However, the various phases of a traŋslation programme, beginning from the selection of a book, ascertaining the competence of the translator and quality of translation, vetting the translation, publication of the translated book, and its distribution, present problems which need careful attention. Not to speak of the adequacy of the various existing academic and non-academic organizations, the sheer lack of knowledge on translation is sufficient to make anyone wary about such a project.

Whether it is translating books into regional languages or writing textbooks in English, very little attention is being given to creative writing. Unless emphasis is given to original research and publication of results, Indians shall always remain junior partners in any academic endeavor. By merely translating books one may at the most know other peoples theories and conclusions well, but one would never know the context of such theory-building and hypothesis formation. It is one thing to be able to get the benefit of technological training, it is another to have a grasp of the scientific research that underlies any such development of the training. The first may be expedient and time-serving, but without the second it does not take any country further along the road of education.

A call for a massive programme for undertaking the translation of textbooks is a step in defence of mediocrity. If the Indian educational system has to be modernized, a critical threshold to be passed through is a drastic change in the attitude: first, of the acceptance of textbooks as the master in classrooms, and second, textbook teaching as the goal of instruction. Instead of these two false attitudes a call for creativity will lead to the single important breakthrough by which not only the seniority system but also the teaching centred education system can be challenged. A sense of competition can be injected and excellence can be accepted as the basis of learning.

'International-mindedness' and 'understanding', acclaimed as goals of education all the world over, are not achieved by the imposition or the adoption of a single language. There is no unanimity on basic issues and fundamental principles among all the English or French speaking countries of the world. In spite of the community of interests of the English speakers of India, the English speaking Brahmin and non-Brahmin of Tamilnadu and

Maharahstra were and even now are locked in a fierce antagonism. Understanding comes from 'learning of the varying ways and traditions, perspectives and purposes' of various people. But unfortunately language politicians in India play on regional sentiment to build up more barriers and restraints and advocate conformity to their respective points of view, rather than; generating respect for each other's language and perspective.

The standard of education is a combination of complex factors. In practice, it may be equated with qualitative education. Academic goals and practices to achieve them, quality of teachers, quality of teaching materials, quality of instruction, all contribute to the quality of education and the setting of a standard. Some academicians in the country raise the bogey of standard in discussing almost anything in relation to education, while they refuse to define goals and take positive steps to free education from the crippling clutches of particularistic loyalties and adherence a seniority system without reference to excellence. Those who are apprehensive of the lowering of standard with a change in language media conveniently forget that there was neither a uniformity of standard among all the English medium institutions nor were all the English medium institutes uniformly superior to all non-English medium institutes. It is generally admitted that a lowering of standard has already set in even with the English medium.

To equate diversity with balkanization, is either foolishness or fanaticism. In the world today conformity is often pushed down the throats of the weak and the underdeveloped in the name of unit. It has set world leaders of education to think. The UNESCO declaration in favour of the fundamental right of the child the world over to develop his own way, the recognition of diversity as the starting point of a healthy education which makes strangers friends, neighbours are results of such thinking. The Greek educationist Ketty A. Stassinopoulou, poses the problem for the sceptics when she writes, 'some may object or express a fear that accepting and respecting differences might well serve understanding, but that it will prevent cohesion and unity, that it will be the end of the different disciplines—social, moral and intellectual—and will, step by step, lead to chaos'. She points out in reply that, 'these fears, based as they are on ethnic beliefs, are terribly difficult to dispel'. While comparing her beliefs of a world unity based on the recognition of basic differences to mosaics, she says, 'Mosaic are, as we know, made of small pieces of glass or store, all different in shape and colour. There is not one exactly like the other. But through the art of lovingly and thoughtfully assembling, with steadfast purpose, these desperate units, the artist has achieved a masterpiece'. If this is true of communities, this is more so of individuals in any educational institution. As Ronbert J. Havighurst rightly points out, 'the good school is thought to be the school that studies its pupils as individuals, and provides for each person variant of the common programme which fits his peculiar abilities, interests, and goals in life'. Thus, the phrase 'attention to individual difference' is a kind of slogan for American education. Through paying attention to differences between individuals it is hoped to secure good quality in education. It is the height of folly to ignore the realities relating to Indian society and education and not to adopt a pluralistic approach to the problems. Once this approach is accepted, the need for proliferation of schools, colleges and universities will be minimized.

A strong plea has been made in favour of the acceptance of the mother tongue as the medium of instruction as far as and as soon as possible. If other Indian languages and foreign languages are used as tool languages, the problem of faculty transfer and communication among peer groups will have been solved. By demanding a certain proficiency in English it can be ensured that people going in for higher education meaningfully manipulate the language. By making English literature optionally available in schools and colleges, the door can be kept open for those who need a psychological satisfaction in developing their aesthetic sense. Acceptance of the mother tongue will not only lead to original research as distinct from duplication or repetition of other people's research, but will give a sense of bearing and self-respect to the scholars.

By teaching in the medium of the regional languages, which will be the majority mother tongue in any area, an opportunity can be created for the common man to participate intelligently in the process of government. It is only natural that regional languages be the vehicle of administration at the state level. For inter-state and Centre State communication a choice of English and Hindi may be judiciously combined which will continue to act as links at different levels.

It is futile to talk and debate about a link language in a vacuum. Today loose and trite terms such as link language, library language, foreign language, world language, ripe language, deficient language, are freely used to mean different things to different people in different contexts. It is often forgotten that as things stand, the mother tongue links the group sharing it in a bond of solidarity. The state language, which is the majority mother tongue in the state provides a linkage among all the linguistic minorities inhabiting that state. Hindi provides a link among a large majority of population of the country irrespective of family affiliation of their mother tongues and English links the educated elites of the country and their peers in other English-knowing countries. Without a proper appreciation of the hierarchical nature of the linkage and the mutual interdependence of languages, language use in education and administration has floundered from one folly to another. Once Hindi becomes the language of instruction and administration in six Indian states, it will provide a powerful motivation to people all India to study the language to increase their job opportunities. The same reason will encourage the study of neighbouring languages by a set of people who want to complete in their vocations in the neighbouring states. This will only put a limited current practice on a more rational basis. Currently a doctor or an engineer moving out of his state does not communicate with his uneducated or even illiterate patient or worker in English, but in the language of the area or in Hindi. By encouraging multilingualism, it will be possible to facilitate and hasten the change.

It is important that the content quantum of linguistics is integrated with the modern Indian languages. It is assumed that unless language pedagogy is discipline based, there is little chance of its scientific development. Modern Indian languages in colleges and universities are mostly taught as the mother tongue. Some universities offer undergraduate, graduate, certificate and diploma programmes in modern Indian languages which are taught as second/foreign languages. In some universities modern Indian languages are use as the media of instruction. In such situations these languages work as the vehicle of knowledge. The introduction of linguistics as an integral part of modern Indian languages courses has to keep these three distinct functions in view. Modern Indian languages courses emphasize the literary content of the language in most programmes. Literature is presented chronologically and the emphasis is more on the history of literature and the pre-literary history of language. Even the literature which is offered is by and large confined to ancient and medieval literature. Most literary research is either text based or author based. Very little attention is given to styles, registers and varieties of the language which fulfil important functional roles.

Some universities have one, two or three papers out of the eight devoted to language and linguistics. Most of such departments are in universities where there is no Linguistics Department. Therefore either a junior lecturer attached to the department teaches the subject or the teacher who is a language M.A. with a special paper or special aptitude in linguistics/language teaches the paper. If one scans all such courses it would be quite evident that in breadth and depth there is much to be professionally desired in these courses. Even in such universities where linguistics is taught as a subject in under-graduate and post-graduate stages there is seldom any dialogue between the teachers of linguistics and languages. The integration of linguistics in modern language courses has to be viewed in this context.

In the above circumstances there is no wonder that even M.As in Indian languages do not have a clear idea about the distinction between the mother tongue, second language and a foreign language, between style and register, language and dialect, language and writing. In spite of the hoary linguistic tradition of the country they have no idea of grammar, language relationship in space and time and the various dimensions of language use in education, administration and mass media. It is therefore, imperative that the objectives of teaching both the languages and linguistics be spelt out before preparing a curriculum either for under-graduate or for post-graduate levels. Whether one is interested in the linguistic study of the language or in the specialization of literature, a foundation course in Applied Linguistics embodying basic notions about language and languages must be given if not at the school stage, at least in the under-graduate stage. Such a course need not be visualized as a different subject but should be viewed as part of the language subject. It is in this perspective that the following observations about goals and strategies are being made:

(a) Language teaching in the schools in defective leading to a gap between language acquisition at the end of the school stage and the language requirement at the beginning of the college level. This is particularly so when one is called upon to extent the domain of the use of mother tongue as the vehicle of instruction and knowledge and as a medium of administration. It is therefore necessary that a bridge course introducing the college entrants to various skills and registers of the language be given on an intensive basis. This should be followed by the inclusion of conceptual prose in the regular under-graduate curriculum.

(b) Language structure and language history need be taught with reference to the language under study. Thus, to begin with, instead of teaching general phonetics and theories of grammar one could teach the phonetics and phonology, and formation and sentence generation, internal and external reconstruction of the language concerned, using linguistic notions.

(c) The development of a rational attitude towards one's own and others' language/dialect, styles and genres of literature can be developed through learning the language system concerned. Thus the basic foundation courses need not be courses in linguistics but would be courses in the Indian language concerned which are based on the discipline of linguistics.

Both under-graduate and post-graduate syllabuses presume that the entry competence of students is uniform. Whether students come from English medium schools or other language medium schools, whether they come with subjects other than language as major or the same or a different language as major, the methods and materials are the same for all. This inflexible uniformity is the cause of many a weakness and need to be remedied.

It sounds strange and yet it is borne out by experience that among those coming to an M.A. with language as an option and language as a mere compulsory subject, the latter perform better. Apart from students opting for the language optional as a last resort, the fact remains that by and large what is taught at the B.A. stage in the optional is irrelevant for the M.A. It is, therefore, necessary to effect better integration among the B.A. and M.A. courses.

The B.A. compulsory as well as the optional courses take the mother tongue competence for granted and concentrate on administering an ambitious dose of literature. Her also emphasis is laid on chronology, author and text. No effort is made to develop advanced skills of comprehension, close study of texts, writing precis, synopsis, narratives, exposition, dialogue and other varieties of prose and acquainting the learner with stylistic variations. The reading of drama and poetry, recitation, which are neglected at the lower stages, could profitably be handled at this stage. These are not antithetic to the study of literature; on the contrary, they are necessary preconditions to the study of literature.

At the post-graduate level, however, there is a need to diversity the teaching of modern Indian languages. One stream in language and another emphasizing literature may be suggested in this connection. In either case the syllabus should be restructured and provide for alternate streams of specialization. It is suggested that there be six core appears and two specialized papers with alternate streams. The six core papers may be: (1) Language use, (2) Language analysis, (3) Language history, (4) Literary analysis, (5) Literary criticism (6) Literary history. Under this scheme grammatical tradition can be handled under the rubrics of language use, language analysis and language history. One can view Paninian grammar, Tolkappiyamor Sabdamanidarpana as efforts at analysing languages of their time. One can also connect and compare that stage with intermediate stages and the contemporary stage, thus studying it under both the rubrics. The alternative streams may be different aspects of the study of literature, some aspect of applied linguistics such as translation, lexicography, contrastive analysis, adult literacy, etc., or some aspects of general linguistics, sociolinguistics and psycholinguistics, etc. The items suggested are illustrative. Different colleges and universities may specialize in areas of their own choice.

Almost all languages and linguistics departments in the country are engaged in preparing dictornaries in one form or another. Yet lexicography as a discipline and a formal course of training has not been reflected in the language curriculum. As a result, most language dictionaries are either poor replicas or adaptations of existing foreign language dictionaries. Very often they do not represent the semantic genius of the language. Specialized training could open up newer vistas and directions to the large number of language M.As, about whose employability questions are raised by those who are responsible for the inadequately trained multitude.

In a multilingual country translation and interpretation present formidable challenges before the language graduates. Very little systematic training facility in this area exists as part of the post-graduate training for those studying languages. The certificate and diploma courses run by some language departments in the area of translation are often not linguistics-based. The theoretical and methodological weakness needs to be remedied in all such courses.

The above recommendations are made on the assumption that language teaching should be discipline-based. Specialization in respect of Applied Linguistics should act as an incentive for students to undertake further study in linguistics. This will also provide linguistic studies in the country the much needed broad under-graduate base. Once the language and literature course, both undergraduate and post-graduate, are linguistically motivated, not only is language teaching in the country likely to be transformed at all levels but also a cadre of linguistically oriented persons could be created who could be utilized for adult literacy and for collecting samples of unrecorded languages and dialects. They could also be usefully employed for a host of other research programmes.

From the above it should be clear that an approach to the curriculum in Indian languages at colleges and universities must avoid the juxtaposition of language, literature and linguistics. The study of each is complementary to the study of the other. The scientific study of language provides a better basis for literary appreciation and a proper study of literature provides a basis for language use in its multifarious dimensions.

While the above programme is designed for those who would take modern Indian languages as subjects of study at the undergraduate and post-graduate levels, there is an immediate need to give a linguistic orientation to those who have already taken such courses and who are engaged in teaching languages in colleges and universities.

The discussion on this subject cannot be complete without reference to the teacher training institutes. The B.Ed, and M.Ed. courses which qualify the persons to teach and man the education departments must be addressed in this regard. Unless the content and methodology of language teaching is drastically modified and updated in the teacher training institutions and the integration of linguistics with the language courses brought about, the very purpose of reform at the college and university level is bond to be defeated. For this purpose it is necessary to organize short-term orientation programmes for teacher-trainees. These should be devoted to studying different aspect of language in teacher training and the problem of integration of linguistics with language courses in the teacher training institutes. In addition, the summer and regular courses suggested for college and university language teachers should also be open to teacher educators.

The underlying assumptions in the above discussion need to be made explicit.

1. An educated citizenry is a must for maintaining democratic values. 'Without an educated public, a democracy', to quote Madison, an American President, 'is either a farce or a tragedy'. English as the medium of instruction, the selective and limited education available to a restricted sector of the society, represents the farcical side. If tragedy is to be avoided,it is imperative that a broad-based universalistic education must be attempted, that will narrow the gulf between the elite and the masses by raising the general level. This is almost impossible to achieve under the present institutionalized schooling.
2. Education is a major social instrument for achieving the twin social objectives of social solidarity and cultural pluralism. It is necessary and possible to recognize mutual differences and generate respect for each other while developing a sense of one nation, one country.
3. The two great enemies of sound education are the absolutism of a monolithic mind and the production of 'people who all go the same way, indifferent or oblivious or even hostile to differences'. Rigidity inhibits adaptation and communication, and standardization leads a human social group to develop as a 'herd without soul'.
4. The non-competitive, seniority based pyramidal

structure of higher education and the accent on particularistic loyalties are the two major reasons for a decline in the standard of education. These coupled with 'want of necessary finance' at the right time and place, and want of determining the correct priority, account for the poor quality of education in India.

5. The adoption of the line of least resistance, the fear of accepting diversity, lack of recognition and respect of the uniqueness of individuals and social groups as a step toward building universalistic education in India, are the greatest faults of the political and academic leadership of present day India.

Education as a state enterprise and universities with autonomy guarantee diversity in education. Since this also gives rise to particularistic loyalty, the Union Government, with purposive planning, can provide checks and balances. As V.V. John rightly concludes, 'In regard to higher education, the constitution lays on the Central Government the responsibility for "the determination and coordination of standards". This is the legitimate role of educational authority in other areas of education too. Besides ensuring that no institution or functionary in education gives short measure to the learning clientele, the role of authority should be to promote innovation and experiment, and make information relating to such ventures available to all institutions so as to encourage a spirit of mutual emulation. This would bring about the true liberation of learning that we are now in urgent need of.'

3

Length of Response

Most students of children's language in the past have been interested chiefly in the extent of vocabularies, that is, in how many words the children has in their active vocabularies. Little interest has been evinced in the way children combine words into word group, and finally, into complete sentences. The simplest and most objective measure of the degree to which children combine words at the various ages is the mean length of response. This measure has been advocated by Nice, who says that it is not the occasional long sentence, but rather the mean length of response, which is symptomatic of the child's stage of linguistic development. Smith, in her study carried on at the University of Iowa, also used this measure and found it a very satisfactory index.

As only the comprehensible responses could be treated according to this analysis, it will be well to consider here the percentage of the children's responses that were comprehensible at each age level. These results appear in Table 1.

It will be seen from these figures, that children's speech becomes increasingly comprehensible with increase in chronological age, that it is almost entirely comprehensible by the age of three or three and one-half years, and that this development occurs earlier in the girls than it does in the boys. Consequently, the number of responses upon which the figures to be reported in the later results are based in larger at the upper levels. The smallest number of responses considered for any age level in this analysis is 260, while the largest is 980 or practically the total number of responses obtained for the age level.

Table

Mean Per Cent Comprehensible Responses

CA	Boys	Girls	All
18	14.0	38.0	26.0
24	29.0	78.0	67.0
30	93.0	86.0	89.0
36	88.0	99.3	93.0
42	95.5	99.8	97.2
48	99.3	99.8	99.6
54	99.6	100.0	99.8

Several statistical measures of the length of response were compared for reliability. They were the mean length of response, the median length of response, the mean of the five longest responses, and the longest response for each child. The last two measures were eliminated because of their large variabilities

It was thought for a time that the median length of response might be a better measure, in this case, because of their large variabilities.

It was thought for a time that the median length of response might be a better measure, in this case, because it seemed that many children used a preponderance of responses of one or two words and had a few very long sentences that would unduly affect the mean. The distributions of the mean and of the median length of response were compared with respect to their reliabilies, not only for the whole experimental group, but within each age group as well.

Although the difference in the reliability of the means and of the medians appears to be very slight, it is somewhat in favor of the mean as a more reliable index. The distributions according to the mean length of response and according to the median length of response and according to the median length of response approximate the normal curve quite closely, especially when we consider that the number of cases involved in only 140. Some children did not talk at all, and so had a zero score for length of response, while some at the upper extreme, had a mean length of response of eight words. This fact might be interpreted to mean that the children used in this experiment were chosen at the proper ages, since with only a few children representing each extreme the distribution is nearly normal. The distribution according to the mean length of response, however, gives a closer approximation to the normal curve than that according to the median length of response. Therefore, in view of the facts that the standard error of the mean indicated that this measure was slightly more reliable, and that the distribution of the mean lengths of response gives a more nearly normal curve, the mean is the measure that has been used throughout the other tables of this chapter.

Table:

Standard Errors of the Mean and of the Median Length of Response for Each CA Group

CA	Mean	σ_m	σ_{mdn}
18	1.2	.022	.035
24	1.8	.055	.038
30	3.1	.067	.078
36	3.4	.068	.088
42	4.3	.091	.094
48	4.4	.091	.086
54	4.6	.094	.096

The mean length of response shows consistent increase with advance in age, with the most rapid, increase between eighteen and forty-two months, and with a much slower increase after forty-two months. This result agree with that of Smith, who says regarding this measure, "There is a steady increase up to four and one-half years, with only small increments of gain after three and one-half years." She reports also that individual curves for children who were observed several times show little or no gain after four years. Further, she says, "This failure to gain after four years and the extreme variability in the older children of the same mental ability make it seem probable that the sentence length as a measure of sentence development has no significance after four or four and one-half years." Nice says that this measure of the mean number of words per response may be the most important criterion for judging the child's progress in attaining adult language.

Table

Mean Number of Words Per Response by CA and Sex

CA	Boys	Girls	All	SD	Smith's Figures		
					Boys	Girls	All
18	1.0	1.3	1.2	.64	-	-	-
24	1.4	2.1	1.8	1.40	1.9	2.4	1.7
30	3.2	3.1	3.1 1	.99	-	-	2.4
36	3.1	3.8	3.4	2.06	3.5	3.1	3.3
42	4.2	4.4	4.3	2.83	-	-	4.0
48	4.3	4.4	4.4	2.86	3.4	4.5	4.3
54	4.6	4.7	4.6	2.95	-	-	4.7
60	-	-	-	-	4.8	4.5	4 .6

It will be seen from the above table, that the results of the present study tend to agree with those of the Smith study, although they run somewhat higher for the group as a whole, especially at the lower age levels, and the sex differences are more marked. Her figures are also lower than those reported by Boyd, Nice, and others, which fact she attributes to the differences in the methods of collecting the data, namely, during "periods of lessened activity and conversation with adults," It must be remembered that this same factor of conversation with adults was operative in the present experiment, but the method in this case should be more reliable since the situation is more carefully standardized.

Sex differences

Contrary the results of the Smith experiment, but quite in accordance with the findings of most other investigators, particularly those of Gale, Mead, Terman, Nice, and Doran, this study reveals sex differences in favor of the girls which, though slight, are consistently in the same direction. There is only one slight reversal, which occurs in an age group in which there was a predominance of girls and in which the boys seem to have been rather highly selected in spite of the careful methods of selection that were used. In view of the consistency of these differences from one age level to another, their relationship to similar differences in the other analyses, and their agreement with the reports of other investigators, they should be considered as suggestive, and possibly significant, even though they do not meet the statistical criterion of the significance of a difference. It will be seen from inspection of the above table, that the differences are greater in the younger age levels at the time when the curve shows the most rapid rise, and that they are less marked in the older children, when development is slower. It seems to indicate that the girls go through the developmental cycle more rapidly than do the boys, but that the boys practically equal them at the close of this rapid developmental period. A similar tendency was noted by Doron in studying vocabularies. He says, "We are not warranted in saying which has the better vocabulary after the twenty-fourth month, though it is possible that further investigation will show the girls surpass the boys up to the fifth or sixth year."

The mean length of response shows interesting trends when considered in relation to paternal occupation. Because of the small number of cases representing the extreme occupational groups, the age levels have been considered in groups of two in this part of the analysis. Table and Fig. indicate a clear superiority of Group 1 over all the other occupational groups in the precocity of this aspect of linguistic development, and the other occupational groups appear in their expected positions at nearly all age levels. It will be noted that there is very little crossing of the curves for the various occupational groups, especially when we consider the few subjects in each group. The greatest crossing occurs in Group VI, which has fewer representatives than many of the other groups, about half of whom were secured through day nurseries or institutions, so that they had other contacts and other opportunities of hearing language outside of the home. Here we have on factor that might account for the crossing of this curve.

The mean length of sentence for Groups I, II, and III, has been compared with that for Groups IV, V, and VI, at the various age levels. As indicated in Table X, the differences between the upper and lower occupational groups for the mean length of response proved to be statistically significant in all but the eighteen-months-old group, in which the number of comprehensible responses involved was much smaller than in any of the other groups.

Mental age

The mean length of sentences has been considered also in relation to mental age. The material on mental age reported in this study has three sources of error. The first is the error in the standardization of the Kuhlmann scale, which was brought out by the Goodenough restandardization, in which it is shown that the Kuhlmann test is too easy at all the ages involved in the study and particularly at the four-year level. It is in error 0.9 of a month of mental age at year two, 0.8 of a month at year three, and 4.7 months at year four. A correction could be made for these discrepancies, but it was not thought worth while in view of the second source of error involved in this material.

The second respect in which this material is in error is that the mental tests were not given on the same date on which the observations of this experiment were made. Most of them were given before the experiment was conducted, and many of them over a year before. The mental ages at the time of the observations on language were calculated by multiplying the CA by the IQ. This procedure assumes the constancy of the IQ and accurate standardization of the test itself. If the correction for the inaccuracies of the scale were made, it would have to be done by using the chronological age at which the test was given and not the age at which the child was classified in this study.

Thirdly, many of the children in this investigation had had more than one intelligence test, and although the second test in somewhat more reliable than the first, the first test was used for all children because only one test record was available for some of the subjects. However, these inaccuracies are not peculiar to this investigation but are practically inherent in the test method as it is used today and hold true for nearly all work that presents material on mental age. Although the chronological age groups are discrete because of the way in which the subjects were chosen with respect to age, it was not possible to have the mental age groups similarly discrete. While the mental age series is really continuous, it has been thrown into class intervals of six months for tabulation, and for purposes of rough comparison with the chronological age groups.

The mean number of words per response for each mental age group is shown in Fig. It will be seen that in spite of this grouping according to mental age, the sex differences still persist in favor of the girls. The mean length of response shows the same sort of curve when considered in relation to mental age that it does when plotted against chronological age until fifty-four months, when it practically reaches a maximum and shows very little increment with increase in mental age beyond the point of maximum chronological age. This is interesting in view of the previously mentioned findings of Nice and Doran.

The differences that were indicated above between the various occupational groups in the mean length of sentence might be due to the different intelligence level that each occupational group represents. In order to test this hypothesis, the mean length of response has been considered in relation to paternal occupation and to mental age as shown in Fig.

It will be seen here that while the differences are not as consistent as in the chronological age table, there is still a tendency for the upper occupational groups to remain superior to the lower groups when mental age is constant. Thus, mental age is probably a factor that enters into the occupational group differences to some extent, but it certainly is not the only factor that is operative.

We frequently hear the belief expressed popularly, and in the scientific literature as well, that the child who associates entirely with adults, or who spends most of this time with children who are considerably older than he, is usually precocious in his linguistic development. The Gales said, "The later children have an advantage in learning must from contact with the older child." This statement is based on the fact that their first child used only one-half as many words as their second and third children at the same age. On the other hand, some people maintain that adults' conversation is so far removed from the child's level that the child can gain little from it, and children are often thought to understand each other much better than they understand adults. One basis for this is the frequency with which twins develop a language of their own, a development which is thought to retard their acquisition of the language of their parents. Hall says, in speaking of children of approximately the same age, "Their noises are too well understood by each other, the younger holding the older back."

This investigation afforded a good opportunity to throw some light on this question. Of course, all children of preschool age associate with adults, but an attempt was made here to discover those children who associate with adults almost entirely, to the exclusion of child playmates. In nearly all cases the mother was asked if the child played with other children, and if so, whether the child's playmates were much older, about the same age, or younger than he. Children who were in day nurseries or in institutions were considered as associating with children about their own ages. In a large proportion of the cases, this information could be obtained first hand, since the other children in the family were frequently seen during some part of the home visit, or the child was called in from play with the children in the neighborhood for the observation.

The subjects of this experiment were all placed in three arbitrary groups on the basis of the ages of their associates. Group 1 includes all children who spent most of their time with associates over twelve years age. Group 2 includes children who, in addition to association with adults, also associate with children who are more than two years older than they. Group 3 includes all children who, in addition to association with adults, also associate with children their own ages or younger; that is, with children who are not more than two years older than they.

These three groups were then considered with respect to the mean length of sentence. Each child was given a percentile rank within his own age level, on the basis of his mean length of response. Then the median percentile rank for each of the above groups was computed. The results of this analysis were as follows: For twenty-seven children whose associates were chiefly adults, the median percentile rank for length of response was 70; for seventy children who associated with older children, 42.5; and for forty-three who associated with children their own ages and younger, 52.5.

Thus we see that those who associate with adults only seem to have a decided advantage in the length of sentence over those who associate with children. The figures for the other two groups, however, are the reverse of the expectations. In order to determine if this difference was due to a pre-ponderance of either sex in either of these two groups that might account for the figures, the number of boys and the number of girls in each group was tabulated. It was found that the sexes were equally represented in each of these groups, so that a sex difference in the mean length of response cannot account for the differences in the median percentile ranks for these age-of-associates groups.

The differences between the occupational groups represent another factor that might be operative in bringing about this result. The tabulation of the number of children in the various occupational groups in each of the above groups revealed the following facts: Of the 27 children who associated chiefly with adults, 13 were from the upper social classes, and 14 were from the lower social classes. Of the 43 children who associated with the children their own ages and younger, 22 belonged to the upper occupational groups, while 21 belonged to the lower occupational groups. Of the 70 children who associated with older children, only 30 were from the upper half, while 40 were from the lower half of the occupational scale. Thus, the upper and lower occupational groups are equally represented in Groups 1 and 3, while there is a marked excess of the members of the lower occupational groups in Group 2 which, no doubt, accounts for the lower median percentile rank of this group of children who associate with older children. In this case we have operating the factor that large families are more numerous in the lower occupational groups, and it is in large families that we most frequently find the preschool child associating with older children. Here again, we have the factor of intelligence operating in the same way as it did in previous instances. The mean IQ for Group 1 equals 113, for Group 2, 106, and for Group 3, 107. There are so many factors involved in the situation and these are so intimately related to each other, that it is difficult to isolate any one of them as the sole factor that brings about such a result. The clear superiority of the children who associate chiefly with adults certainly is not due either to the sex differences, or to the occupational group differences. It does seem to be related to intelligence, but probably the important factor that functions here is that the situation in which the data were collected was that of talking to an adult which, no doubt, placed those who were accustomed to associating chiefly with adults at a decided advantage.

Bilingualism

The factor of bilingualism is another problem about which there has been a great deal of speculation, but about which few facts are known. Since 10 per cent of the children in this study heard a foreign language in the home, it seemed advisable to study them in more detail. The numbers involved here are too few to allow any conclusions to be drawn, but the tendencies found are suggestive and indicate some other problems that might be attacked by a method similar to that of the present study.

The median percentile rank on the basis of the mean length of response for the 14 children who heard a foreign language in the home was 40. This is only slightly below the central tendency of the group as a whole and is especially surprising when we consider that 9 were boys, and only 5 were girls. Again this result is surprising when we note the tabulation of these cases according to paternal occupation as 2 belonged in Occupational Group 1, 2 in Group II, one in Group III, I in Group IV, I in Group V, and 8 were members of Group VI. This indicates that it is the extreme groups that hear a foreign language, and that over half of the occurrence of bilingualism is in the sixth occupational group. Table shows the median percentile rank according to the language heard.

Thud it appears that in spite of a predominance of

boys and a great overweighting of the lower occupational groups, bilingualism does not seem to be a serious handicap in linguistic development as measured by the mean length of response. However, this does not mean that it is not a handicap to proper pronunciation and construction. All we can conclude from these meager data is that the hearing of a foreign language in the home does not seem to be a handicap in linguistic development as it is measured by the mean length of response, which, when applied to larger groups, has proved a very reliable index.

Mean Lengths of responses in order of occurrence

In order to determine the extent to which shyness entered into the experimental situation, the mean lengths of the first ten responses, of the second en, of the third ten, etc., were calculated. It was expected that shyness would exhibit itself by a tendency to shorter responses, and that any tendency for an initial shyness to be overcome during the period of observation would be indicated by this series of means for the responses taken in groups of ten, in the older in which they were recorded. The figures for this analysis for all age levels together are shown in Table

It will be seen from this table that the children's responses tended to be somewhat shorter at first, but that there is little change in the mean length after the first ten or twenty responses. The mean for the initial responses for the girls is relatively lower than it is for the boys, and the maximum level is reached more slowly by them than it is by the boys. This result would seem to indicate greater shyness among the girls of the group, as is evidenced by shorter verbal responses.

Time required to obtain fifty responses

The length of time that was required to secure fifty responses from each child was recorded at the time of observation. This varied greatly with the individual child, as the range for the length of the observation period was from seven to fifty minutes. The mean length of time for recording for each age level and by sex in shown in Table.

It will be noted that the mean time required for observation changed very little with chronological age. This is due to the fact that while the younger children say very little and have long materials between their responses, the older children talk much more, use longer sentences, and give more elicited responses. These factors seem to operate to balance each other, so that the length of the observation remains fairly constant at the various age levels, although there is a slightly tendency, which is more marked among the boys, for the older children to have a shorter observation period. No consistent sex difference appears in this series of figures, which may mean no sex difference in shyness if the measure of the length of time required to obtain fifty responses is considered an index of shyness. The time required to secure fifty responses gave a correlation of -.203 with the total number of words used by each child and a correlation of +.126 with the percentage of elicited responses for each child.

4

Method and Reliability

Purpose

The present investigation is an attempt to add to our knowledge of the development of the language of the child, as it is found in samples of the running conversation of a large number of children selected so as to give a random sampling of the population. The function of language in the child's life, the change in the length of sentences, the complexity of sentence structure, and the proportion of the various parts of speech that occur in the material, are the chief aspects of the problem attacked in this investigation.

Collection of data

1. *Age.*—On the basis of several indications in the literature, it was decided to include in the present study children between the ages of eighteen and fifty four months. While many writers report that children talk much earlier than the lower age limit of this experiment, it must be remembered that most of the reports in the literature are records of children of the professional class and are records of the most precocious members of that group. Eighteen months was taken as the significant age at which to begin this study of sentence formation, since it is the age at which the most advanced children begin to combine words.

Many writers report that by five years the child's conversation is so fluent that an accurate record of it fro any great length of time is almost an impossibility. Nice reports that the development of the sentence is practically complete by fifty-four months, It has not at that time reached the degree of perfection found in the adult, but the period of its most rapid development is over. It thus seems that in considering the language development is over. It thus seems that in considering the language development of the small child we are dealing with a function which develops very rapidly during are pre-school period, and which varies greatly from one individual to another as the time of its appearance.

For the present study, therefore, twenty children were selected at each of seven age level of 18, 24, 30, 36, 42, 48, and 54 months, making a total of 140 subjects. These seven groups were absolutely discrete as t age, as each child was observed within a month and a half of the age at which he was classified. This method of selection meant that a child was classified. This method of selection meant that a child who was born on April 15, 1923, had to be examined between March 1 and June 1, 1926, in order to be included in the thirty-six-month-old group. The greatest discrepancy included was one of forty-eight days, and there were only four cases in which the deviation from the proper date for examination was more than forty days. An effort was made to have these deviation from the proper date for examination was more than forty days. An effort was made to have these deviations not in excess of two weeks for the children at the deviations not in excess of two weeks for the children at the two youngest age levels, where development is most rapid.

In such a rigid stratification of age levels, this study differs markedly from previous investigations, particularly from that of Smith, who examined the children first without regard to age and classified them later into convenient intervals, which in most cases were whole-year age groups. In her study, a three-year-old subject was any child between the ages of two years and six months, and three years and five months, so that her age groups were really not discrete but continuous. When we are dealing with a function that develops as rapidly ad does the child's language, it seems that whole-year age groups are so large, and have so much variation within them, that the stages of the developmental process may be obscured.

2. *Paternal occupation*: In order to make the experimental group representative of the preschool population of Minneapolis, the occupation of the father was used as a criterion of selection. The Barr-Taussig sixfold classification of occupations, used by Goodenough, was applied to the adult male population of Minneapolis between the ages of twenty-one and forty-five years, and the percentage in each type of occupation was calculated from the census report of Minneapolis for the year 1920. These figures, together with the corresponding ones for the experimental group, are shown in Table 1.

Table I

Mean Deviations From Proper Date for Examination

Age Group	Deviation in Days
18	+2.9
24	-4.5
30	-.9
36	+1.3
42	-1.8
48	-3.7
54	-.7

The subjects of the experimental group were carefully selected so that these socio-economic classes were represented in their proper proportions, not only in the group as a whole, but within each age level as well. Similarly the two sexes were approximately equally distributed in the entire group and in each age group.

3. *Intelligence*: Mental test records, nearly all of which were based on the Kuhlmann Revision of the Binet Scal, were available on 95 per cent of the subjects.

The mean IQ for each age group is decidedly above 100, as in shown in Table III. However, this does not mean that the group is as highly selected as the figures seem to indicate, for it must be remembered that Kuhlmann's original standardization gave average IQ's of 108, 106, 107 for the ages of two, three, and four years, respectively. The corresponding figures from the Goodenough restandardization of the Kuhlmann scale are given in the same table. It will be seen from a comparison of these figures that in spite of the rigid method of selection used in this study, in an attempt to secure a random sampling of the preschool population of Minneapolis, the experimental group was slightly above the average in intelligence at each age level. This tendency, it will be seen, is more marked in the girls than it is in the boys, which is in accordance with the findings of Goodenough and others. up is shown in Table IV, together with the corresponding figures from the Goodenough study. It will be seen that while in general they seem somewhat higher, they are in the same order of magnitude except for the one high mean of Group II.

Although the method of selection used in this experiment is the best that we now know, certain unknown selective factors have been operative in spite of our precautions, which might bring about the slightly higher intelligence rating of these children. One of the factors is the cooperation of the parents. No parents refused to allow observation of their children for this experiment, but the families with whom contact was made were largely either those whose children were members of the control group of the Institute of Child Welfare at the University of Minnesota, and who had been brought to the Institute at least once for mental examination, or those who had availed themselves of the opportunities of the free clinics of the Infant Welfare Society of Minneapolis. These two factors probably operated to make the selection somewhat too high. A similar factor was operative in the opposite direction among the members of the lower occupational groups, since they were recruited chiefly from institutions and from the clients of social agencies. A third of these factors is the greater stability of the population from which the subjects were selected, since only those whose address were the same for several months, or a year, were available for observation. Thus, while we still have some errors of selection, they tend to counterpart each other, and the experimental group in this study is probably as good a sampling as it is practically possible to secure.

Table

Mean IQ by Paternal Occupation

Occupational Group	This Study	Goodenough
I. Professional	118.1	116.1
II. Managerial	121.0	111.7
III. Clerical	112.0	107.7
IV. Skilled labor	105.9	105.3
V. Semiskilled labor	106.4	104.3
VI. Unskilled labor	100.3	96.0

Method of observation

Each child was observed individually in his own home or in a place very familiar to him, such as a room in the Nursery School or in one of the day nurseries of which the child was a member. Whenever possible, the child was alone in the room with the examiner, but in making home visits this condition was often difficult to control. In many cases the mother was present during all or part of the observation, and this circumstances often put the child more at ease. Occasionally, other members of the family were present as well, which factor usually stimulated the child's conversation rather than hindered it.

Fifty consecutive verbal responses were recorded for each child exactly as they sounded to the experimenter. This number was decided upon because it would give a fairly representative sample of the child's stage of linguistic development in a relatively short period of time, without tiring the child with a prolonged observation. A response was considered as a separate unit if it was marked off from the preceding and succeeding remarks by pauses. A complete sentence was always considered as single response, but a response was frequently less than a sentence. The responses were recorded exactly as they sounded to the experimenter, even in the cases of the youngest children, many of whom gave verbal responses that were entirely incomprehensible. However, these children have many sounds in their vocal repertoires for which we have no adequate written symbols; and hence, any attempt to record their utterances in writing is very unsatisfactory. Such responses have been treated separately, and only accurate result they yield is the number of syllables combined per response. In some cases of peculiar articulation, the mother's interpretation was considered if it clarified the child's speech, and if it was obvious that she was giving a literal reproduction and was not elaborating on what the child had said. It was surprising, however, in how many of these cases the mother was quite frank in admitting that she understood the child no better than did the examiner. The record did not include recitation of nursery rhymes from memory or responses uttered in direct imitation of another person.

In order to overcome self-consciousness and to establish rapport, the child was shown picture-books and toys, which usually were quite effective as an introduction. The same set of toys was used throughout the experiment.

One of the picture-books contained pictures of animals, usually with one central object in each picture. This book was particularly suitable for the younger subjects, who could not comprehend the group relations is more complicated pictures. Another book which was used, and which was more suitable for the older children, contained group pictures illustrating various Mother Goose rhymes. The toys used where a little red auto, a cat that squeaked, a telephone with a bell, a little tin mouse, a music box, and a small ball. The toys were not presented in the same order to all children. Frequently, the older children were asked whether they preferred to look at toys or picture-books first. A preference was usually indicated, but if not, the experimenter presented the toy that seemed best suited to the age, sex, and apparent interest of the child. If it failed to bring forth any verbal responses after considerable inspection on the part of the child, another toy was tried. Sometimes a child became so fascinated with the first or second toy that the quota of fifty responses was obtained without the presentation of other toys. Some of the children, on the other hand, fitted from one subject to another so rapidly, and with so few comments, that the whole series was gone through several times before the desired number of responses was obtained.

Since the aim was to secure spontaneous responses, the child was addressed as little as possible during the observation. In the cases of some quiet, shy children, it was necessary to stimulate conversation to some extent, but an effort was made, in such cases, not to use questions that could be answered by a single word. If the child's response was brought about by something the examiner or the mother had said, it was recorded as an *elicited response* and, where necessary, he remark of the other person was also recorded verbatim. This method of recording differs from those used by Piaget, Smith, and others in three ways: first, the child is talking to an adult, rather than playing with children; second, the same amount of data is obtained for each child; and third, the situation is more nearly the same for all subjects. Piaget and Smith observed the children for a definite period of time during free play in groups with other children. The situations differed greatly from one child to another, for in some cases the children were engaged in active play outdoors, while in other cases they were engaged in quiet, indoor play in which conversation was much greater in quantity and probably different in quality. In observing children for a definite length of time, as was done in these other studies, very few data were obtained from some quiet, shy subjects, while a tremendous amount of material was obtained from the talkative ones. It seems that it is better to compare equal samplings of children's language responses recorded in similar circumstances, even though the situation may not be entirely natural.

In the Piaget study and in the Smith study, the person with whom the child conversed was different for each observation, and often changed during an observation; whereas, in the present study all the children conversed with the same person, thus standardizing this aspect of the experimental situation.

Other data obtained for all the subjects of the experiment included: the length of time required to secure the fifty responses; the time of the observation; the nationality of the parents, if they were of foreign birth; whether or not the child heard a foreign language in the home; the age of the child's associates; and whether the child had lived chiefly in the home or in an institution.

Analysis of data

In any attempt to deal with data of this sort, one is immediately confronted with a great many difficulties. Everyone who has tried to understand the chatter of little ones realizes from this usual observation how difficult it is to hear the child's words correctly. Children of eighteen and twenty-four months vocalize a great deal, and whether we understand them or not, we cannot afford to ignore these important stages in their linguistic development. Even children who can be readily understood most of the time, frequently use words and phrases hat are entirely unintelligible to the hearer. It was necessary, therefore, to divide the data of this experiment into: (1) *comprehensible responses*, which included all responses that could be understood by the experiment in spite of poor articulation, letter substitutions, or faulty or incomplete construction; (2) *semicomprehensible response*, which included all responses in which the hearer had a general idea of what the child was talking about but could not get the full meaning because of the lack of certain key words in the sentence; and (3) *incomprehensible vocalization*, which included all responses which were mere sounds forming no recognizable words, and which were entirely devoid of meaning to the hearer. These responses included three sub-groups: (a) *single sound* (b) *repetition of the same sound, or babbling*; and (c) *series of varied sounds*.

Analysis according to the length of response

The only quantitative treatment of these data in terms of equal units that is possible, is the analysis according to the length of response. The semicomprehensible responses and the incomprehensible vocalization were scored according to the number of syllables combined per response, while the comprehensible responses were scored by the number of words per response. In attempting to count the number of words in a response, many problems arise as to what is to be considered a separate word and what combinations are to be counted as one word. In order to overcome these difficulties and to standardize this part of the scoring system, it was necessary to formulate a set of arbitrary rules, as follows:

1. Contractions of the subject and predicate like "it's," "we're," "you're," etc., were scored as two words. In such cases the child speaks correctly according to adult conversational usage, which really is his only model of correct speech. Each part of the contraction is as essential part of the sentence, and if the sentence is to be considered complete, it is necessary to recognize these two parts. In order, therefore, to make the analysis according to the length of response consistent with the later analysis according to the construction of the response, it seemed justifiable to seem such contractions as two separate words.

2. Contractions of the verb and the negative like "can't," "won't," etc., were scored as single words. The child who has no knowledge of how words are written does not know that "can't" is a contraction of "can" and "not." He hears "can" as one word and "can't" as another; they have different meanings and hence are probably two distinct and independent words to the child.

3. Hyphenated words and compounded nouns, particularly proper nouns, which are not hyphenated,

but which probably function as single words and as names of single objects, were scored as one word. Example, "merry-go-round," "Mother Goose," "Betty Lou," and such expressions were scored as single words.

4. Each part of a verbal combination was scored as a separate word. For example, "have been playing" counted as three words.

5. "Lookit," which occurred frequently, was scored as one word if it was used alone and functioned simply as "look." If, however, it was followed by an object, it was counted as the two words "look at."

Functional analysis

Language is the foundation of all our social relations, for it is the primary medium by which we communicate our ideas and meaning to others. Dewey says that the primary motive of language is to influence the activity of others. Its secondary use is to enter into more intimate social relations with them, and the third and final use of language is in the acquisition of knowledge. Thus, this important aspect of the child's language develops in relation to the needs of the child. In considering the linguistic development of the young child, we should concern ourselves not only with its increasing length and complexity of structure but with its function in relation to the child's environment. What situations in which the child is placed bring about language responses? We find the young infant very early expressing himself in gestures, but when he begins to substitute verbal responses for his overt bodily responses, which overt responses are first superseded by verbal responses? In what situations does speech first appear? Piaget considers this a problem of functional psychology which indeed it is. Sometimes, he says, language conveys information, sometimes it provokes action in others, etc. This is an important aspect of the linguistic development of the young child that heretofore has been quite neglected. The old grammatical classification of sentences into declarative, interrogative, imperative, and exclamatory sentences is a crude analysis in this direction, which serves fairly well for written language, less well for adult conversation, and is quite inadequate when applied to the speech of children. As Claparede so aptly says in the preface of Piaget's book, "In examining child thought, we have applied to it the mound and pattern of the adult mind."

So often a sentence is structurally of one kind and functionally of another; there is so much overlapping of the categories; and so many subheads would have been necessary to make it meet the demands of children's conversation, that the rigid grammatical classification of sentences was abandoned in the present study. The function of the child's response in relation to his environment was considered the important thing in this type of approach. Practically the only attempt at treatment of this sort, that is available in the literature, is that of Jean Piaget of the Jean Jacques Rousseau Institute at Geneva. He says in the introductory chapter, "We have aimed first and foremost at creating a method which could be applied to fresh observations and lead to a comparison of results." This method has filled a serious need in the present study very satisfactorily, and has been adopted with certain modification in the functional analysis of the data. Modifications of the classification were made necessary by the different circumstances under which the observations were made, by the use of much younger subjects, and by the desirability of subdividing some of the larger categories for a more detailed analysis. All of the comprehensible responses were scored according to this functional analysis, which, as modified for the present purposes, consisted of the following categories:

A. Egocentric speech

1. Repetition or echolaia
2. Monologue
3. Dual or collective monologue

B. Specialized speech

1. Adapted information
   (a) Naming
   (b) Remarks about the immediate situation
   (c) Remarks associated with the situation
   (d) Irrelevant remarks
2. Criticism
3. Emotionally toned responses
4. Questions
5. Answers
6. Social Phrases
7. Dramatic imitation

By *egocentric speech* Piaget means that in which the audience is disregarded. The child "talks either for himself or for the pressure of associating any one who happens to be there with the activity of the moment." He "speaks only about himself and makes no attempt to place himself at the point of view of his hearer." In this study this category includes instances in which the child speaks about persons and things other than himself, but in which he disregards an audience. The three types of egocentric *speech* are defined as follows: *Repetition or echolalia* means "repetition of words and syllables....for the pleasure of talking, with no thought of talking to anyone, nor even at times of saying words that will make sense." *Monologue* occurs when the child "talks to himself as though he were thinking aloud" without addressing anyone. In the third type, called *dual or collective monologue*, "an outsider is always associated with the action or thought of the moment but is expected neither to hear not to understand. The point of view of the hearer is never taken into account. He presence serves only as a stimulus... The child talks about himself without collaboration with his audience or without evoking a dialogue."

Socialized speech occurs when the child addresses his hearers, or considers his point of view, tries to influence him, or actually exchanges ideas with his hearer. The first category of socialized speech according to Piaget is *adopted information*, in which the child really "exchanges his thoughts with others, either by telling him something that will interest him, influence his actions, or by actual interchange of ideas." It occurs whenever "the child adopts the point of view of his hearer, and when the latter is not chosen at random." This group was found to include such a large proportion of the conversation obtained in this experiment, that it seemed advisable to analyze it is more detail. The first subgroup that appears to be quite distinct is that of *naming*, in which the child announces the name of an object either as a single word or in a complete sentence. The second type includes all *remarks about the immediate situation*, other than naming. The third group is made up of all remarks that are not about the immediate situation but are logically related to it, i.e., where the observer can see the connection between events or remarks in the situation. For example, if upon presentation of a toy auto the child said, "It's a auto," the response would be placed in the naming group. If his next remark was, "It's got a spare tire," this remark would belong in the second type of adapted information, or the remarks about the immediate situation. If the succeeding remarks were, "I have a car like that," Mine's broken," they would be additional information volunteered by the child, which was obviously brought about by the situation and associated with it, and hence belong in the third type of adapted information, or *remarks associated with the situation*. The fourth type of adapted information consists of *irrelevant remarks*; that is, those in which the observer cannot notice any connection with previous remarks or actions.

The second type of socialized speech in *criticism*, which includes "all remarks about the work or behavior of others, but having the same character as adapted information," according to Piaget's definition. In the present analysis, this classification was extended to include criticisms of objects as well as that of persons and also complaints about situations in which the child is thwarted.

In the third group of socialized speech, Piaget includes all "commands, requests, and threats." For the present purposes, this category has been extended to include all wish-words or "Wunsch-wortes" as Meumann terms them—in short, this group includes all *emotionally toned responses*. Single-word sentences uttered with a decided emotional or commanding inflection are also included in this group.

The fourth group consists of *questions*, by which are meant real interrogative sentences with an interrogative function and declarative sentences having and interrogative function, i.e., any remark that definitely requires an answer from the hearer. It does not include declarative sentences with a question added at the end merely for affirmation or approval of the statement and requiring no answer on the part of the hearer, as "I made it go, didn't I?"

In the fifth group are included all *answers* that are "answers to real questions and to commands." In this study the category includes all of the elicited responses. However, remarks occurring in the course of conversation and having the form of answers, but which are answers to remarks that are not questions, are not placed in this category but rather under adapted information.

A sixth category has been added to Piaget's classification to provide for the *social phrases* which occur only in social situations, but which the child has been taught to say parrot-fashion, and which probably function as single words to the child, such as, "please," "thank you," "you are welcome," "bye-bye," etc.

The last group of socialized speech is called *dramatic imitation*, which consists of all talk in imitation of the conversation of adults, like imaginary imitative telephone conversations. It also includes imitation of the sounds made by animals, like "bow-wow-wow," "meow," "moo-moo," and the imitation of the sounds of automobile horns, etc. Probably Piaget would put such remarks in one of the categories of egocentric speech, but while many such remarks might the placed there, some of them are used in decidedly social situations and in social contexts, and hence this classification has been provided for them in this study.

Construction analysis

We have now outlines two methods of analysis of these data, both of which consider the response as a whole. The first was a quantitative analysis based on the length of response and the second was a functional analysis of the response according to this relation to the child's environment or to the total situation. Three is still another important aspect of the development of speech that must be considered. This is an analysis according to the construction of the response, which attempts to indicate the stage of grammatical complexity that the child has reached, or in other words, how closely his sentence structure approximates adult conversation, his sole criterion upon which to model his speech.

The first and most obvious way to classify responses of this sort is to throw them into the dichotomy of *complete* versus *incomplete* sentences, and these are the two main groups of this type of analysis. However, in a preliminary perusal of these data, one is impressed with the frequency of responses that are incorporate sentences. Ordinarily, we think that we speak in complete sentences, and that the sentence is the essential unit of language. A superficial analysis of a small sample of adult conversation is sufficient, however, to show that a larger proportion of our conversation is composed of phrases and other groups of words that really do not constitute sentences according to the grammarian's definition. Very often the whole sentence is merely implied or "understood" as the grammarians, say, but it is not expressed in its full form.

True, the adults understands that a verb and a subject belong in a sentence, and were he to write the same statement, he would use the complete form. But the child knows nothing of written language; his sole pattern and criterion of correctness of language is the conversation of the adults with whom he associates. If a response is adequate in the situation, and is what an adult would say in such circumstances, the child is using the most complete form that he has had an opportunity to learn, and therefore, in this study such responses have been classified separately as one type of complete response that is *functionally complete but structurally incomplete*. This group, then, includes practically all the single-word sentences and most of the elicited responses or those belonging in the answers group of the functional analysis. The outline of the classification used in this third type of analysis is as follows:

A. Complete Responses

1. Functionally complete but structurally incomplete responses
2. Simple sentences without a phrase
3. Simple sentences with a phrase
4. Compound sentences
5. Complex sentences
6. Elaborated sentences

B. Incomplete Responses

1. Omission of the verb
2. Omission of the subject
3. Omission of a preposition

4. Omission of a conjunction
5. Omission of the verb and the subject
6. Miscellaneous omissions

The titles of the second, third, fourth, and fifth categories of the *complete responses* are quite adequate and need no further explanation. The sixth classification, *elaborated sentences*, however, represents an interesting type of response that it seems advisable to include as a separate group. In scoring the responses of some of the oldest children, it was noticed that they often used long, involved sentences that really were much more complex and seemed to indicate a higher stage of linguistic development than the ordinary compound and complex sentences, which, in some cases, may be quite short. This classification was added, therefore, in order to differentiate these more involved responses and to see if they proved diagnostic of a more advanced stage of development. This group includes sentences with two phrases, two clauses, or a phrase and a clause.

All responses that were incomplete functionally as well as structurally were scored as *incomplete*, and the type of omission was indicated. The major groups of omission are shown in the above outline. Other combinations of omissions occurred but not with sufficient frequently to warrant separate analysis. These, therefore, are the groups that are included in the miscellaneous omissions. Since in recording children's speech it is often difficult to be sure whether or not one hears the articles, omissions of the articles have been disregarded. If a sentence was complete except for an article, it was considered complete and no penalty was inflicted for its omission, since its absence might have been a function of the recording and not a true omission on the part of the child. It was possible to give construction scores only to comprehensible responses and to the more complete of the semicomprehensible responses. Thus, we have outlined three types of analysis that deal with the response as a whole, namely: the length analysis, which is quantitative; and the functional and construction analyses, which are qualitative.

Word analysis

In addition to the above-described analysis that consider the response as a whole, it was thought advisable, particularly for comparison with the numerous vocabulary studies reported in the literature, to conduct a more detailed analysis by considering the parts of the response. Hence, although the primary purpose of this study was to study the development of the sentence and to consider the response as a whole, a word analysis has also been conducted. The vocabulary reports in the literature are much more thorough than that of the present study, in that they are based on more complete samples of each child's vocabulary. However, these studies have all been of two or three children, all at different age levels, so that data for comparisons of children of the same age, and for tracing the changes from one age to another, are very meager. This word analysis has been conducted merely to see if small samples of the vocabularies of a large number of children would confirm the reports of the complete vocabularies of a few children, and in order to suggest possible tentative, normative material on the proportions of the different parts of speech at the various age levels. As mentioned in the preceding chapter, there are nearly as many ways of counting children's vocabularies and for determining the proportions of the various parts of speech as there are writers on the subject. However, Bateman's rules for counting words and for determining the parts of speech seem to have met with favor from the other authors, and since they have been used in three or four other studies, they have been applied in the present instance. They are as follows:

1. Include no proper nouns
2. Include no plural form unless the singular was not used.
3. Include all forms of pronouns
4. Include no variants of verbs or of adjectives unless they are from a different root.
5. The same word may be listed more than once according to its grammatical use; i.e., if a word is used as a noun and also as a verb, it is included twice.

The frequency of occurrence of each word was found as well as the total number of words, the total number of different words, and the percentage of each part of speech used at each age level.

5

Language in Elementary Education

Language plays an important role in the early childhood education in any educational system. A language is not only taught as a subject but is also used as the medium of instruction for teaching different school subjects right from the beginning. Thus, a language teaching is charged with additional responsibility for teaching different skills of the language and making the child able to use this language as the medium of learning other school subjects. Though the special role of language in the early childhood education is not defined, yet no adequate attempts are being made in schools for helping the teachers in fulfilling their responsibilities. Teachers must be aware about certain broad aims and specific objectives of language teaching and must be able to adopt appropriate teaching strategies. In this chapter, an attempt will be made to outline some broad aims and objectives of language teaching in early childhood education and to suggest some strategies to be adopted by the teachers depending on language teaching and learning situation with special reference to India.

There are certain fundamental values which a language teacher of the elementary education must understand before preparing to teach the language. A language teacher must be acquainted with the linguistic and socio-cultural background of the child. A child comes to school with his own vocabulary and a set of tools for expression. He already uses language as a form of communication at his individual level and communicates with the members of his family, children and others in his own unique way. His early experience with the language must be recognised as a basis for the built up of skills. The particular structure of child's family must be recognised as an integral part of the educational continuum. Since all individuals are different, a teacher must accept the fact that each child develops his faculties or capabilities in his/her own way on the basis of his/her exposure to various experiences. A teacher must recognise the fact that due to the factors given above, all the children are basically different, they are to be treated differently and individual attention must be paid in enriching their language experience.

Keeping the basic values in view, broad aims of language teaching in elementary education must be drawn along the following lines: (a) setting up an appropriate environment conducive to language learning, (b) providing adequate opportunities for the child to use the language and develop his self expression, (c) developing the child's ability to communicate in different social settings, (d) enriching the child's language experience, and (e) developing all the skills necessary for the actual use of language. We need to develop these objectives keeping in view the possible teaching and learning situations.

It is very important to set up an appropriate environment inside the classroom or school in which a child is encouraged to develop skills of language. A child must get ample opportunities for listening and speaking. It is essential to provide materials suitable in the classroom/school which a child can make use of. Various activities must be aimed to add to the child's experience. It would be necessary to know what interests the child most, and what stimulates him/her to use expressive skills of speaking and writing. The learning environment must help him to develop the spoken language and creative thought. A child will feel free to communicate and share his/her experience with others in a stimulating environment of classroom/school. The child must never feel alien in the environment and must feel himself/herself a part of it. An alien environment will hamper his progress in developing the skills of language independently.

An innovative teacher can adopt different strategies in making the environment stimulating for the child to develop his skills of language. Some of these basic principles must be followed: (a) Materials which are displayed in the classroom and provided for the use of child must be of the child's level and interest. They may include photographs, wall pictures, posters and other raw materials which can be easily handled by the child. The child must have an easy access to these materials (b) The displays used in the classroom must be attractive, meaningful and relevant to the activities carried over in the classroom. For example, words which occur in the poems/stories recited or narrated in the class can be written on the posters. Pictures can be used to illustrate the meanings of some words. The child while listening a piece of poem or reciting it can look at the words and 'read' it with the aid of visuals. (c) Materials used for the class may be of various kinds. Materials made of paper, clay, wood, steel etc. can be used as models. Various kinds of materials including parts of objects may be kept at the disposal of the child to make his own things in the form of blocks, pictures, drawings etc. (d) All the items in the classroom must be labelled in legible words, captions in the form of small sentences can also be used. (e) The space available in the classroom can be divided in different areas for the development of language skills. It should be possible to have an area for reading materials and an area for listening and another area for language games. (f) A teacher has to present himself/herself a very suitable model for imitation in both listening and speaking skills. A teacher must listen attentively and respond to the child appropriately when he is talking. The teacher must give proper attention to *what* the child is saying and not on *how* he is saying. It has been observed that the child feels more interested and involved in the conversation of one who talks with him at his/her eye level. (g) A teacher must try his/her best to provide encouraging stimulus and positive feedback. (h) The environment provided in the classroom must prove helpful for both the child to learn the skills of language and for teacher for imparting experience in the actual use of the language.

A child must be provided adequate opportunity to develop his self-expression with confidence. His self-expression will be developed if he is encouraged to express his personal thoughts, ideas and experiences through language. A teacher must realise the relationship between the development of one's personality and the development in the use of language skills. Personality development and language development are considered to be interwoven. For the development of self-expression, objectives must be help and encourage the child clearly express his thought, ideas, experiences and feelings through language. It is equally important to develop the child's confidence in the use of the language.

Difference teaching strategies can be adopted for the development of the self-expression of the child. A teacher may make use of child's photographs, photographs of the members of his/her pets. A child can talk about a photographs freely. Some such materials which provide subject matter for talking must be provided by the teacher.

Children may be encouraged to act in plays in different roles. Plays can be made more interesting by providing different costumes. Children may act in small stories, render dialogues and imitate characters. Children must be provided adequate opportunity for talks and discussions. They can talk about different flowers, clothes, pictures classroom objects, classmates etc. Children will feel more at home with describing familiar things. They can describe these items in detail. Pictures which are drawn or collected by a child can be compiled together with the help of the teacher. The child's description of these pictures can be written underneath each picture. Different language games can be introduced by the teacher in order to develop child's self-expression.

Main objectives of the development of the ability for social communication are (a) to help the child learn to share his knowledge with others, (b) to develop the ability to convey and receive ideas, thoughts and feelings, (c) to help the child learn to put across his ideas, and (d) to help the child develop the ability to listen to others and respond with confidence. The child must be given adequate opportunity to interact with his peer-group and adults. This would enable him develop his ability to express his thoughts and feelings to others. A teacher must keenly observe the interactions which take place in which a child is involved and make sure that a child gets ample opportunity to develop his social communication.

A teacher will have to make sure that each child is given the opportunity to participate in conversation. Each child must be given an opportunity to discuss, to ask and answer questions. Each child must be given opportunity to listen and be listened to, to offer and receive explanations.

A teacher can adopt different teaching strategies for developing the ability of a child in social communication. A teacher may develop the technique of asking open ended questions so that language is used not only as a medium of communication but also as a tool of thinking. A teacher may make use of visual aids like a number of pictures and involve children in discussing them. Conversations may be recorded and compiled. Children may play different social roles and act according to the situations.

Different forms of literature-fiction, poetry etc. enrich the child's language. The child's language is also enriched by his direct experiences of tours, picnics and observations. different audio visual aids such as records, cassettes, tapes, pictures, slides etc. also enrich his experience in many ways.

Main objectives of the developing of language experience are: (a) to develop in the child an interest and appreciation of language through different form of literature, (b) to help the child respect books and to make him/her aware that books are used to acquire knowledge, and (c) to help the child develop an appreciation for different forms of literature and enjoy the beauty of language, and (d) to help the child realize not only how the spoken word can be realized as written word, but also how to enrich spoken language with the help of written form in different situations.

A teacher is to play a crucial role in developing the language experience of the child. He may adopt different strategies towards this end. A teacher has to select interesting books and arrange them in an attractive manner in a book-corner in the classroom. He has to involve the children in arranging these books in the manner which suit them so that they find it easy to locate the books of their choice. The selection of the books will depend primarily on the interest and level of the children who will make use of them, and also the objectives a teacher has in mind. The books read in the classes are to be discussed by the children under the supervision of the teacher.

A teacher must inculcate an interest in the child for borrowing books from the library and also encourage parents of the children to help him choose books in other local libraries etc. A teacher will also read and tell stories to the children; he must ask the children to summarise the stories they have heard or read.

A teacher must read stories and recite poems from the books and encourage children imitate him in the recitation of the poems. Stories poems which are read in the class must be discussed by the children. New words and ideas need to be discussed and understood properly. The books which deal with the famous paintings and art objects are of special interest to the children. Children must be encouraged to tell their own stories. Their stories may be recorded and played back so that children are encouraged in narrating their own stories.

In short, for the development of the language experience, a teacher has a very crucial role to play. It largely depends on the training of the teacher and his own experience, understanding, and innovations which help him in devising different types of suitable teaching strategies keeping in view particular teaching and learning situations.

In the early childhood education, emphasis is to be laid on the development of receptive and expressive skills. Main objectives of receptive skills are to help the child to develop the ability to comprehend what he hears, observes and reads. A child should be able to listen accurately and read with comprehension. a child should be able to follow the directions. Main objectives for developing expressive skills are to develop the child's ability to express himself clearly in logical sequence, and to increase his/her vocabulary. A child should be able to clearly express his thoughts through oral and written expression.

A teacher may adopt different teaching strategies for developing these skills. Selection and graduation of teaching materials, audio-visual aids and teaching techniques to be adopted by the teacher will play a decisive role in achieving the targets.

In a country like India, problems concerning the teaching of languages in early childhood education are immense. Though adequate time id allotted for the teaching of languages in the elementary schools, but language teaching is not done in the right sense of the term. Language teachers are not properly trained in the teaching languages. Teachers' Training Colleges have not given adequate attention to the subject of language teaching. In the absence of a regular pre-service training programme for language teachers hardly understand the problems of language teaching and are not aware of the main aims and objectives of language teaching. Aims and objectives of language teaching must be clearly drawn and the language teachers must be trained in the language teaching methods.

Another important problem is the non-availability of adequate number of suitable books for children. As our current language teaching in schools is primarily based on the test-book teaching, a child is supposed only to read the prescribed textbooks. Most of the text-books prescribed for school children in Indian regional languages suffer from a number of lapses. The materials given in the text books are not language-oriented. In other words, they do not help the child learn different language skills. The materials are not properly graded. A teacher 'teaches' the text with the help of explanation/translation and expects his students to remember or memorize the explanation/ translations. The aim should be to teach the skills of language and not a particular text-book in translation. In the elementary level, we require to develop different kinds of materials which are language skills-oriented. The so-called 'text-books' need to be re-written by skilled language teachers must be supplemented with different types of drills and exercises suitable for a particular language teaching situation. Well graded books must be made available on different forms of literature for the children at different levels. These books need to be written for children alone and not down to the children, as is the current practice.

As discussed above adequate efforts need to be made in providing an appropriate language environment in the schools. Emphasis must be laid on the development of child's self-expression, his ability of social communication, his language experience and the basic receptive and expressive skills. There is a great scope for the development of suitable language teaching materials and language teaching techniques.

6

Language in Teaching Situations

The notions of mother-tongue, first language, second language and foreign language have been defined and discussed in detail. As far as language education is concerned, they are to be understood in terms of different language teaching and learning situations.

The mother-tongue is the language naturally acquired by the child from the early family atmosphere and environment the child is first exposed to. The mother-tongue is distinguished from the first language. The first language can be the mother-tongue of the child but it need not always be so. The term 'first language' is usually associated with the native language of a speech, community, region or a state, where it is used for wider communication and may be used in education, mass media and administration.

The language taught in its natural environment to the native speakers of the language is indeed a first language teaching and learning situation. When the same language is taught to the non-native learners of the language it is categorised as second language teaching and learning situation. In the second language teaching situation, the language learning does not actually remain confined to the classroom only, there is a continuous re-inforcement from the environment outside the classroom. The second language learners learn the language faster when taught in its natural environment. When a language is taught in an alien or 'foreign' environment or, in other words, when the teaching and learning of the language remains confined only to the classroom and there is no immediate re-inforcement from the environment, the language teaching and learning situation is characterised and a foreign language teaching and learning situation. As far as language education is concerned, foreign language does not necessarily be the language of a foreign country. Thus, it is the actual teaching and learning situation which assigns different labels to various languages in education.

The mother-tongue has an important role in education. This is language primarily used in concept formation and creative thinking which are important aspects of language education. In the words of Pattanayak, 'Mother-tongue is the language with which one if emotionally identified. It is the language through which one expresses one's basic needs, ideas, thoughts, joys, sorrows and all other things. This is the language which if one gives up and adopts another language, one may become intellectually alive but grow emotionally sterile. The primacy of the mother-tongue has been established by the educationists and applied linguists alike.

The choice of language to be used in education, mass media and administration is determined by various factors. Teaching of Indian languages in various language teaching situations have given rise to a number of issues related to language education. Some of these issues are explained with the help of examples of Hindi and other regional languages.

Generally, Hindi is identified as a first language of a speech community in which any regional variety of this language is spoken natively. Most of the regional languages in the country are limited to compact and geographically well defined areas. The Hindi regional language area is spread over vast geographical area. Seven Indian states—Bihar, Uttar Pradesh, Madhya Pradesh, Delhi, Haryana, Rajasthan and Himachal Pradesh have recognised Hindi as the regional medium for all the purposes. Hindi has been declared as the official language of the country alongwith English and is supposed to replace English in due course of time.

As compared to other regional languages of the country, the regional dialects and other varieties which are now broadly classified under the label of Hindi have discernible variations in pronunciation, grammar and vocabulary. Some varieties of this language are spoken in geographically widely separated areas. Apart from the regional dialects such as Braj, Awadhi, Bhojpuri, Rajasthani, Maithili etc. which are rich in literary tradition as well, a multitude of conversation styles, called by numerous names like Hindustani, Khariboli, Dakhini Hindi or Dakhini Urdu etc. are spoken in different social situations and under different prestige conditions.

In Urban areas, a speech community in Hindustani or Hindi-Urdu developed as a result of the language contact and mixed glossia. The development of modern standard languages—Hindi and Urdu began in the early nineteenth century. With the urbanisation and the development of mass media and communication, the spoken Hindi-Urdu variety in the urban areas has gained a social prestige. The native speakers of this standard Hindi-Urdu variety still represent a minority. This variety is popular among the urban groups, the people who have migrated from different rural regions where other dialects or varieties of this language are spoken. For a larger number of people, the standard variety continues to function as a second speech style. This style is used only in certain social situations.

The study of the standard variety in schools, the medium of formal education, the official status and the social prestige of this language have largely contributed in transforming regional varieties of the language into the commonly accepted norm of registers of speech in urban areas.

Hindi and Urudu are not considered very distinct in structure for a serious linguistic study. According to Kelkar Hindi and Urdu consists of the gamut of integrated variations that need to be studied together with a single framework. Kelkar has further pointed out that the case of Hindi and Urdu is a matter of diglossia rather than of dialectical variation. Baring a limited domain of varieties known as High Hindi and High Urdu showing 'horizontal diglossia' mainly in respect of lexical stock, writing system and literary heritage, the rest of Hindi-Urdu is a case of simply 'vertical diglossia'.

In Hindi language area, Hindi plays an important role in education, administration, business, mass media etc. As an official language of the country, envisaged by the constitution, Hindi has to play an important role and has to acquire competence as an expression of all the elements of the composite culture. As per Article 351 of the India Constitution, 'it shall be the duty of Union to promote the spread of Hindi language, to develop it so that it may serve as a medium of expression for all the elements of the composite culture of India and to secure its enrichment by assimilating without interfering with its genius, the form, style and expressions used in Hindustani and in the other languages of India specified in the VIII schedule, and by drawing wherever necessary or desirable, for its vocabulary, primarily on Sanskrit and secondarily on other languages'. Keeping in view these objectives, one would expect that functional roles of Hindi must be emphasized in the curriculum of the language. The need-based varieties of Hindi represent diverse field of professional or social activities of the society.

As indicated above, Hindi has a pan-Indian character and it is taught as a first language in seven states. It is also taught in most of the other non-Hindi regional states right from the primary level upto the University level as a second language. The instructional objectives and the curricula used in different situations hardly show any significant distinction. Teaching of Indian regional languages in various academic institutions share some common problems regarding the instructional objectives, curriculum designs, instructional materials, methods and strategies in different language teaching and learning situations.

After independence, most of the Indian regional languages are taught in their native regions right from the primary level upto the university level. Mostly the academic institutions offer literature-oriented courses. Various forms of literature such as poetry, prose, drama, principles of literary criticism and history of literature etc.

are represented in the syllabi of these languages. These literature-oriented courses invite criticism or various grounds which in part is quite justifiable. Mostly, there is an emphasis on the teaching of ancient and medieval literature and no serious and adequate attention is paid towards the teaching of contemporary literature. More emphasis is given to teaching *about* literature than really teaching literary sensibility and critical judgment. There is no proper curriculum planning for the teaching of language and literature in most of the courses.

The study of language and literature are to be equally emphasized under language teaching. These two aspects need to be distinguished from one another. The present day courses do not make any distinction between the two. Generally, current curriculum does not provide an opportunity for the teacher to teach the structure of the language, its various uses and to build a skill of literary appreciation, critical acumen and value judgment. Text books and traditional grammars, wherever they are used, teach *about* the language and literature. It is imperative to distinguish between the teaching about language from the teaching of the use of language. The teaching of the use of language should come first for second foundation.

An important question to be considered is whether the linguistic-oriented course and the linguistic textual analysis help in refining the literary sensitivity of the learner and help in sharpening the learner's power of interpretation. Primary responsibility with the teaching of literature is not to teach the literature but to impart a skill in the recognition and comprehension of various literary values of the works. Students should not merely be expected to swallow the pre-digested opinions of the earlier critics as value judgments. the extrinsic values of the literary pieces reveal the historical, socio-cultural and political settings of the society, their influences on the author and his background and interests. It is only by a thorough study of the literature with literary sensibility, comprehension and value judgment, the learner will understand the intrinsic and extrinsic values of literature. The study of the language of literary text must be related to a general description of the language. The study of the literature and the study of language must be brought closely together.

Language is used in different dimensions. Different uses of this most powerful medium of communication need to be taught and learnt. Language as a medium of literature is generally studied in the context of textual analysis. Literature as a creative expression in language, presents only literary use of the language in the forefront. All other dimensions of the use of language do not find a place in the curriculum for language teaching in this courses. Educational institutions are expected to build a command of the language in the learner in all its dimensions. The 'command of language' is regarded as 'the ability of mature, educated native speakers to exercise full control over the environment by means of their language behavior'. For building the command of the language in the learner, it is important to teach both literary and non-literary uses of the language. The present curriculum in Indian languages does not provide a place for the non-literary uses of this language. Different registers, specialized uses of the language in different fields of human activities, must form compulsory part of the language teaching. The use of language in scientific and technical subjects, business, literature, mass media—radio, television, films etc. are marked by certain distinctive features. All these registers of the language must be included for study in curriculum for a language.

The objective for the first language teaching and learning need to be distinguished from those of the second language teaching and learning. The curriculum used in different educational institutions does not make any distinction between the two. For example, the contents of the courses in Hindi used in Hindi regional language area and non-Hindi regional language areas are more or less same.

The aims of the teaching of a particular language need to be examined thoroughly and objectively. There is adequate relevance for teaching of a native language in the school curriculum. It is not sufficient to teach about the correct usage of patterns using prescriptive methods. The interference of regional varieties in the standard form may result in the production of unacceptable utterances. The students must be made aware of these variations and taught how the language works. They need to be taught the distinction between the spoken and written varieties of he language should be presented. The students need to learn how to use their native language in the most effective way. It is unfortunate that the new linguistic concepts, methods of analysis, and description of language do not have many practical applications in the teaching of languages in educational institutions. The language teacher must go beyond his text books and prepare himself with the sources of information about the language. The study of linguistics will help the language teacher in reshaping his ideas of language and language teaching. The linguistically-oriented language courses will enable a teacher to teach all the skills of the language and language use in different dimensions. Only a trained language teacher should be able to use the graded language teaching materials effectively.

The teaching of a first language can be improved by specifying the instructional objectives, designing an appropriate curriculum, gradation of text-books, evolving new techniques of evaluation and testing and teacher training. Instructional objectives for first language teaching need to be specified clearly. It is desirable to make students aware about the regional and other dialectical variations of a language. At the initial stage, only the standard variety of the language may be taught in the class. In most cases, children have contact with the standard language in the classroom only. The variety of language they speak at home and in the neighbourhood may be different. Special efforts by way of repetitive drills and systematic reinforcement are necessary for developing the habitual response in the standard spoken variety. Emphasis must be on developing all the basic language skills among the children as listening, speaking, reading and writing.

Although it would be helpful for the teacher to know the native variety of the language spoken by his students at home; he should, however, use only the standard variety of the language in the classroom and outside the classroom. The instructional objectives should emphasize the use of standard variety of the language as the medium of instruction in other school subjects also. It is desirable to teach both literary and nonliterary uses of the language. Different registers and styles of the language used in certain professional spheres and other social situations may be taught. The functional roles of the language must be emphasized and the students must attain a command of the language in all its dimensions.

An appropriate curriculum for the teaching of a first language must be designed keeping all the instructional objectives in view. Table points out that 'the scientific curriculum development needs to draw upon an analysis of society and culture, studies of the learner of the learner and the learning process and the analysis of the nature of knowledge in order to determine the purposes of the school and the nature of its curriculum'. With an objective for teaching both literary and non literary uses of the language, the curriculum design must indicate the details of the course, and demarcate the areas to be covered under a particular course. The contents of the course may be determined keeping in view the socio-political, national, cultural and economic factors. The curriculum design for the language concerned should provide sufficient guidelines both for the text-book writers and the teachers.

An important task for the curriculum designer should be to specify the overall plan for the learning process including the items and components at different levels of the course. While including the learning items in the curriculum, enough justification must be provided for selections from ancient, medieval and modern literary items keeping in view the instructional objectives of the course. In a language-oriented course, more emphasis should be on the teaching of literary sensitivity and interpretation of contemporary writings. The curriculum format for the courses in a language taught at different levels will certainly be different, but it should not ignore the instructional objectives.

Gradation of the teaching materials forms an important task for language teaching. The materials set for a particular course in language must be graded very carefully. The NCERT report on curriculum planning states that on the one hand the content should be graded on the basis of the degree of unfamiliarity, complexity, abstractness and the sequence inherent in the content itself, and on the other hand difficulty level of the expected behaviours under the instructional objectives, the changing interests and the mental level of the learner also influence it. The gradation of teaching materials in the first language teaching involve sequencing the teaching items and components of different language skills, contents of literature, registers and styles. For improving the language skills, it is important to grade the materials in terms of syntactic complexity. Attempts should be made to move from simple to complex structures. The teacher's experience and training, the learners' background, the level of course, and instructional objectives will determine an appropriate gradation of teaching materials.

No proper attention is paid to the need for imparting in service training to the teachers who are qualified to teach a first language in the schools. It is thought that nay nature speaker of a language can teach his language in a school and no special training is necessary for teaching one's own mother-tongue. It is a very false assumption. Lack of teachers' proper training is a great handicap and the methods of teaching cannot be improved without giving emphasis on the teachers' training. The language teachers need to reshape their ideas about language and language learning. A teacher need to understand the instructional objectives set forth for a course of study. A teacher should have enough knowledge of the structure of language, its background and context for students language activities. Only a trained language teacher should be able to use linguistically-oriented language text-books, graded teaching materials and design tests to fulfill the instructional objectives of the course.

Learning of mother-tongue or first language and learning of a second or foreign language need to be distinguished. A child learns his mother-tongue in its natural environment in his early childhood. No special efforts are necessary to teach the basic patterns of mother-tongue to the child. Whereas special efforts are necessary in teaching or learning a second or foreign language at different levels. A person learns a second or a foreign language when he (1) masters the sound system of the language, understands the speech, and is able to speak, (2) learns the use of grammar of the target language, (3) learns adequate vocabulary of the target language, and (4) is able to understand and use expression of the language in different contexts and situations.

A second or foreign language teacher has to use different instructional materials and employ different methods for teaching the target language at different levels. The selection of instructional materials and methods of language selection of instructional materials and methods of language teaching, the use of audio-visual aids etc. will depend on various factors such as the language and cultural background of the learners, their age and the aims and objectives of the language course.

There are certain general and common principles which are necessary in all the situations in second or foreign language teaching. A second or foreign language teacher has an important role to play in providing a good model to his students to copy. A teacher has to make a right selection of the instructional materials which would interest his students from their functional point of view. A teacher has to keep in view students' primary interest in learning the language and select materials accordingly. A teacher has to provide himself a good model of spoken language to the learners. Students likely to imitate the teacher's pronunciation to the maximum possible. He has to help his students to acquire an acceptable pronunciation of the spoken target language and correct their mistakes. He may use language laboratory lessons and other recorded materials as well. He has to provide a model of the culture of the people who speak the target language natively. He may use different audio-visual aids for explaining different cultural bound items and situations. A teacher needs special training in second or foreign language teaching which would help him in the preparation and selection of appropriate instructional materials, audio-visual aids and in presenting a good model for his students.

A second language learner of the language is supposed to master all the four basic skills of the language. The learner must acquire the skill of listening before he attempts to speak. He should be able to listen with clear understanding. It is a skill which needs to be taught and learnt. Once the learner is able to recognise different speech sounds, words, and utterances, he has to develop the skill of speaking as accurately as possible following a good model. The skill reading will involve mastering of different types of this skill—i.e., laud reading and silent reading with understanding. Special reading materials with proper guidance will be acquired for the purpose. The writing skill is to be acquired with the help of properly graded teaching materials and the skill does not merely expect the learner to know the writing system of the language but he should be able to express himself as clearly as possible and develop creative writing skill.

A language learner receives the knowledge of all the four skills at different levels of learning and fixes the knowledge in his memory. The instructional materials and the teacher's guidance help the learner in these steps. The learner is not to merely receive the knowledge in different situations and contexts, the basic skills in language learning are of two types-receptive and expressive. His receptive ability can be measured by the speed and correctness with which he understands whatever he hears and reads in the language. Similarly, his expressive ability can be measured by the speed and correctness with which he is able to speak and write. Various language teaching methods and instructional materials to be used by the teacher and efforts put in by the learner are equally responsible for acquiring of all the skills in language learning.

The results of the applied linguistic research have provided a sound basis for the practical task of language teaching. The application of linguistic research in this direction has resulted in the production of new teaching materials and different kinds of teaching aids.

The teacher's role, both in the classroom and in the preparation of teaching materials has changed to a large extent by introducing new objectives, methods and teaching aids. The introduction of the new methods in the language teaching demand the specialization on the part of the modern language teachers. The teacher is required to have sufficient knowledge both in and about the language he teaches. The language teacher must have acquired a high level of proficiency in the language, theoretical knowledge of its forms and structures and must have an adequate knowledge of certain underlying disciplines, methods and techniques of the language teaching. The teacher should be in a position to analyse new courses, text-books and to produce the teaching materials, keeping in view the aims of the language teaching and the teaching aids available to him. It is important that a second or foreign language teacher should be in a position to analyse the mistakes of the learners at phonetic, morphological and syntactic levels. While giving the pronunciation drills, the teacher must have an adequate training in phonetics for analysing mistakes of the student accurately and for explaining the correct production of sounds. Similarly, the teacher must be in position to explain different phonological, morphological and syntactic structures of the language he is teaching. In order to specialize in the techniques of the instruction, the modern language teacher must undergo an intensive training in accordance with the objectives of the educational system, the methods of instruction and the teaching aids available.

It is needless to say that the teaching methods used for the mother-tongue or first language teaching have to be different from the methods to be used in the second or foreign language teaching. In the second or foreign language teaching, it is desirable for the language teacher to have as far as possible the knowledge of the structure of pupil's mother-tongue. This helps the teacher in analysing the mistakes of the learners and in explaining the structural similarities and/or dissimilarities between the learner's mother-tongue and the second or foreign language he is learning. This question is much debated that how much role does one's mother tongue play in the learning of a second or a foreign language. The second and foreign language teachers are aware of this interference, and wherever possible attempts are made to produce the teaching materials keeping in view this fact. It is considered that a constant conflict between the structure of the foreign language and the structure of the learner's mother-tongue does exist in the mind of the learner. The degree of this interference varies due to factors including the age, level of awareness of the mother-tongue and previous language training in the mother-tongue and/or in any other second language. It has been suggested that the language teacher should select the phonemic and grammatical patterns and lexical items in the target language courses in accordance with similar and dissimilar items in the system of the mother-tongue of the learners. While designing the courses, the teachers should emphasize the common and distinguishing features of the mother-tongue and the target language, at different linguistic levels.

Aims of the language teaching are largely determined by what particular educational system requires, and what the learner demands. Language teaching has undergone considerable change keeping in view different aims. Earlier, main aim of the language teaching was an aspect of literary and cultural education. Now the main aim is considered to be imparting of practical ability in the use of the second or foreign language in communication

In the language instruction, in view of the new methodology, efforts are being made to place more emphasis on the actual speech of the language. The learners are provided those lexical items and structural patterns which are as natural to the every language as possible. It is only after mastering these basic structural patterns of the language, the learner may study and use other complex lexical items and structural patterns for any different reason. For instance, if an educational goal is to learn the literature in the second or foreign language, the learner will meet different problems and has to familiarize himself with various literary styles and expressions. He has to study various socio-cultural aspects of the people and other historical developments in the literary styles which might have taken place. Therefore, the learning of a foreign literature is well understood only after the learner has acquired an advanced linguistic knowledge of the language. The learning of language is of a different nature and necessarily precedes the learning of literature in the language.

In a situation where the second language is taught in its natural environment or, where there are adequate chances for the learner to use the language outside the classroom too, intensive oral courses prove helpful at the early stage of the language instruction. The natural environment, or residence offers advantages in many ways. The learner gets a change to live and act in natural ways and uses the language he learns as the medium in natural conversations in the surroundings.

7

Language Teaching Methods

Different kinds of language teaching methods have remained in vogue and are being practised in different language teaching and learning situations. Some methods known under the labels of 'Grammar-translation method', 'Direct method', 'Linguistic method' etc. are being generally talked about whenever language teaching methods are discussed. We will briefly review some of these methods here and point out the appropriateness of language teaching methods in different types of actual language teaching and learning situations.

The Grammar-translation method was remained in practice for a long period of time in second or foreign language teaching situation. Under this method, teacher lays emphasis on the teaching of the grammar of the target language separately and also on the translation of selected text from the target language in the source language. In General, the teacher lectures his students in their native language on the grammar of the target language, allows his students little or no opportunity to use the target language and seldom uses it himself. Students are required to recite or memorize conjugations of irregular verbs, but he seldom hears or speaks any real sentences in the target language other than the examples provided as illustrations of grammatical points. Pupils are taught definitions of the parts of speech and are expected to memorize conjugations, declensions and other rules of grammar. The teacher teaches the translation of selected pieces of text, and pupils are encouraged to translate with the help of bilingual dictionary or glossary. A great deal of class time is taken up by translating the daily lesson into the student's native language. A student is seldom asked whether he really understands the passage/lesson he is translating. After years of study is this method, students are unable to carry on conversation in the language. The ability to translate is not the same as the ability to understand, speak, read and write—the four basic skills of language learning. Similarly, the ability to talk about the grammar of the language and to recite its rules also does not help in attaining the above four basic skills.

Under the 'direct method' an attempt is made to make the direct contact with the target language in meaningful situations. The idea of this method is to associate the words and sentences with their meaning through demonstration, dramatization and actual size. This method thus de-emphasizes translation and does not encourage students to merely memorize conjugations, declensions or other rules of grammar.

This method was largely practices during 1920s and 1930s especially at commercial language teaching schools. Under this method teachers as well as students are strictly forbidden to use anything but the target language. A teacher tries to engage the students in free conversation, illustrating the meaning by means of gestures etc. The subject matter of the conversation is planned in advance so that students concentrate on a certain type of vocabulary etc. It is not possible to control grammatical structures and sentence patterns. A student is exposed to a bewildering range of sentence patterns. Since this method advocates the natural and functional use of the target language, grammatical explanations and grammatical drills are avoided.

The direct method generally develops a passive understanding of the language and the learners are able to carry on conversation in the language only in the limited number of situations and they cause only limited number of structures. This method fails to build up the four skills of the language adequately.

The linguistic approach to language teaching has resulted in the emergence of several methods of teaching and learning of different skills of the target language. It is argued that four languages kills—listening or understanding, speaking, reading and writing are to be taught in the same order in the second or foreign language situation. The emphasis on the first two skills-listening and speaking, has given rise to a particular method called 'audio-lingual method'. This method is used for teaching the skill of listening or understanding as well as the skill of speaking. The learners should be able to understand the spoken language properly and they should be able to speak it adequately. The 'audio-lingual method' is used for the two oral skills in language teaching. Similarly, the use of linguistic approach has resulted in the developmental of different techniques for the teacher of the two other skills—reading and writing.

The linguistic approach is helpful in making the learners conscious about the structure of new linguistic system and they are encouraged to master the system by adopting different methods. For teaching through this approach, the teacher should have an adequate knowledge of the linguistic structure of the language and should be able to present himself as a good model for imitation and acquiring of acceptable pronunciation. The emphasis on pattern practice under this approach helps to build the habit of actual usage of sentence patterns in learners rather than the memorization of individual sentences taken from the text.

It is well established that most important differences between any two languages are not those of lexical items or words, but of structures. Each language has its own system of phonetic and phonological structure, sentence structures and patterns. The learner must be able to keep the two linguistic systems apart and make conscious efforts in mastering the new linguistic system i.e. the target language. The goal in learning a second or foreign language is to acquire ability to understand the speech and writing of natives of target language by listening and reading respectively and to be able to use the expressive skills of speaking and writing which are acceptable to the native speakers of the language. This implies that the language learners must be able to understand the meanings and connotations of the speech and writing of the target language, and be able to use the expressive skills of the language in its target cultural context.

As pointed out above, the skills of listening and speaking come first the order of language learning in this approach learning in this approach. The 'audio-lingual method' is based on the same principle. In the next step the skills of reading and writing are to be acquired. The learner should be able to read with comprehension. Writing is the graphic representation of the language and does not represent intonation, rhythm, stress and junctures etc. It is only after mastering the skills listening and speaking, a learner will be able to read with comprehension and master the skills of writing gradually.

The choice of a particular language teaching methodology actually depends on particular language teaching and learning situation. The situation is determined by the aims of language teaching or learning, linguistic background of the learners, are and motivation of the learners, the teacher's capability etc. Whatever the teaching and learning situation is, there are some general factors or principles of language teaching and learning which cannot be ignored in any situation. Some of these important factors are briefly discussed here.

A learner has to imitate a good model of speech for acquiring an acceptable pronunciation. Speech cannot be invented by the learner, it has to be imitated. A teacher has to make sure that he provides a good model of speech for the learner's imitation. A good model does not guarantee good imitation, but it is necessary for a learner to imitate and the learner has to make best efforts in imitating the model as accurate as possible.

Under a linguistic approach, instructional materials in the form of conversational dialogues are generally preferred in the beginning. Sentences structures and vocabulary items of the target language introduced in the lessons must be properly graded. Conversations prove suitable in presenting sentence structures in cultural context and the learners feel themselves involved in the live conversations. The use of the free prose or poetry is not appropriate in the beginning of the course. Prose makes little use of questions, requests and answers. Longer statement patterns at this stage are not helpful. Similarly, poetry makes use of more unusual constructions and the less typical variants of common constructions.

Conversational lessons in the beginning help the learner to acquire the sentence patterns in a habit through pattern practice. The learners must learn to use them in the proper context. The learners must be able to use the patterns of construction of the language with appropriate vocabulary at normal speed for communication. A teacher has to be careful in grading the materials and in introducing them.

The use of mere translation in the beginning is not desirable for several reasons. Only a few words, if any, are fully equivalent in meaning in any two languages; the learner considers words equal in meaning and commits errors when he extends the translation to the same situations as in the original; and word-for-word translations generally produce incorrect constructions. It is not possible to achieve good translation skills without mastering the target language. Language teaching must precede the teaching of translation as a separate skill. Translation is a skill which needs to be taught after the learner has acquired adequate command over the target language. Translation is not an appropriate method for language teaching. A bilingual, who has acquired two co-ordinate linguistic systems does not translate one into another, but uses any one system independent of the other.

Some variables such as age, educational level, capability, level of proficiency, goals, linguistic and cultural background of the learner are very significant. A language teaching course needs to be designed keeping in view all these variables. These variables also help to determine the suitability of a particular language teaching methodology in a particular situation. For example, children and adults must be taught a second or foreign language differently. The teacher may have to teach the language to the learners in any of the following age-groups—pre-school, primary school, secondary school, college, university, and other adult groups, Pre-school children can learn a second language by exposure in much the same way as they learnt the first language. These children will learn the second language if these are brought in contact with appropriate situations in which the second language is used as a medium of communication. No other special technique is necessary to teach the children at this stage. They learn mostly by play and memorization. Children can achieve very accurate pronunciation by war of their power to mimic speech sounds accurately and by using the language in communication. At the secondary and above levels, special techniques are necessary to be employed in teaching the new linguistic system and by using graded instructional materials.

Keeping in view the goals of language teaching, conscious efforts are to be made by both the teacher and learner in achieving the objectives. The preparation and presentation of instructional materials are very important in any teaching and learning situation. Conversational dialogues must be useful ones which can be drilled with interest. The learner must develop the power to hear, recall, understand and speak the dialogues with ease. Conversational lessons written on some functional subjects exemplify in a natural way different types of questions, requests, statements and the use of vocabulary that constitute the language. Shorter dialogues are more useful than the lengthy ones, as dialogues in most of the situations are learnt by miniory-memorization technique. Some dialogues are automatically memorized by the learners and they feel free to use these dialogues with expansions or alterations in different situations. Technique of drills is very important in the presentation of materials. It is observed that group recitation must precede individual recitation. This order of drills offer clear advantages. In the beginning, student feels less inhibited in a group response; he recites more readily, and gets a change to practice every part of the lesson. The students response in both group and individual recitation must be lively and varied in speed and volume in as natural a manner as possible.

As mentioned above, the choice of a particular language teaching method largely depends on the teaching and learning situation which include different variables. There seems to be general agreement among professional language teachers that an eclectic approach must be adopted in an ideal language teaching and learning situation. A language teacher must be prepared to adopt an appropriate technique depending on the actual situation.

A sentence and not a word is considered as the smallest unit of full expression. Words are part of the sentences and by themselves they do not constitute full expression. Each language has a restricted number of structures and patterns of sentences. We may define a structure as a sentence framework of which the basic features remain constant while allowing for extension and changes and substitution of words as per context. For example in the framework of the structure "He is a........", a variety of content words relating to occupations may be substituted, e.g. doctor, lawyer, writer etc. Also, we may use other subject pronouns and the corresponding parts of verbs; we may also change it to interrogative or negative as well. Each of these variations is called a sentence pattern. Thus each structure may involve a number of sentence patterns. Students who learn the language must be able to use all the patterns.

Drills and exercises constitutes an important part in any language teaching and learning situation. Drills are administratered orally and can be of various kinds like repetition, substitution, build-up, expansion, transformation, response etc. Generally, cues are provided orally and the learners use these cues in the models given for drill whenever necessary. A teacher can use different techniques in administering drills in the class. Drills reinforce the learning of particular grammatical structures and enable learners to practice the actual use of language.

There is a wide scope for the trained language teacher to innovate and use different techniques in administering drills. Exercises are written assignments for the learners. Exercises provide an opportunity for the learners to apply their knowledge of the language acquired independently. Exercises given in the language courses can also be of various kinds. Some common exercises useful for the language learners are those of fill-in-the blanks, completion, transformation, combination, questions on the text, usage of lexical items and phrases in sentences etc.

A teacher's responsibility in any language teaching and learning situation is to follow the most appropriate method in introducing the lesson, administer drills in the most effective manner, correct the written assignments and remove the individual or collective problems or learners.

As stated above, there need not be any rigidly as far as the choice of a particular language teaching method is concerned. It is important that a teacher is aware about different methods of language teaching which would enable him to make the best choice of a particular or an eclectic method keeping in view in actual language teaching and learning situation.

8

Learning about Verbal Referential Communication in the Early School Years

Introduction

If children are to use their linguistic skills to their best advantage, they must know about the requirements of effective verbal communication and the causes of communication failure. One important cause of communication failure is message ambiguity: speakers may give messages which convey their intended meanings ambiguously. If they do, listeners may make an incorrect interpretation, and if a correct interpretation is to be guaranteed, listeners must be given more information. Data collected by a number of researchers using a variety of procedures and methods of analysis, are consistent with the view that children of around 5 commonly do not conceive of the process of communication in this way. These children may make an incorrect analysis of the reasons for communication failure and may not take appropriate action to solve the problem. As a consequence, they may not use their linguistic skills as effectively as they might either as listeners or as speakers. By the age of about 7, many children seem to have acquired an accurate conception of these aspects of the process of verbal communication.

In the next section of this chapter, 'Age-related Differences in Communicative Performance and in Understanding about Communication', we shall specify these changes which occur between the ages of about 5 and 7 years, and in the third section, 'Identifying Causes of Change in Understanding about Communication', we shall begin to identity features of children's social world at home and at school which could explain these changes. We begin by summarising descriptive data which illustrate how younger and older children *perform* as speakers and listeners in various referential communication tasks, and also how they *judge* both message quality and the cause of communicative success or failure. In many respects young children are often effective communicators by the time they go to school; their performance as speakers and listeners shows that they can use certain strategies which contribute to communicative success, and their judgments show that they are aware of some of the characteristics of good and poor messages. However, our emphasis will be on the deficiencies of younger children as compared with older ones, since we are interested in developments which take place in the early school years.

Age-related differences in communicative performance and in understanding about communication

In practice it is not always easy to distinguish between children's listening or speaking performance, and their judgements about messages. For example, in some studies in which the focus of attention is upon children's responses to ambiguous and unambiguous messages, children are explicitly told to point to the correct referent when the message is unambiguous, and to make some other response when the message is ambiguous. These could be seen as nonverbal judgement tasks, but they differ from straightforward performance tasks only in so far as children are explicitly told what to do when the message is ambiguous. We shall include studies such as these in the next subsection on performance data, and we shall reserve the following subsection for data concerning children's verbal judgements.

Children's performance as listeners and speakers

Typically in investigations of children's performance as speakers, they are asked to describe verbally one of a set of items so that a real or imaginary listener could identify it. The set of items might be, for example, pictures of triangles which differ in size, pattern or colour, or they might be toy people wearing and holding different articles. In some studies the speaker's task has been more complex, e.g. to instruct a listener how to complete a model. In either case, to be an effective speaker the child must convey an intended meaning unambiguously by purely vocal means.

Child listeners in investigations of performance are typically asked to interpret ambiguous and unambiguous verbal messages. When the message is unambiguous, they are expected to point to the referent or carry out the instruction. When it is ambiguous, they are expected to ask for more information, or indicate in some other suitable way that they have identified the message as inadequate.

The results of studies such as these show that as speakers, younger children are likely to give ambiguous messages even though they have the vocabulary necessary for giving unambiguous ones. As listeners, they commonly interpret ambiguous messages as if they were unambiguous. These findings are reported by, for example, Alvy; Cosgrove and Patterson; Ironsmith and Whitehurst; Whitehurst and Sonnenschein; Patterson and Kister; Robinson.

These characteristics of young children's listening and speaking performance suggest that they respond to ambiguous and unambiguous messages in much the same way. There are, however, some respects in which they respond differently to ambiguous and unambiguous messages. For example, Bearison and Levey found that children who made incorrect verbal judgements of ambiguous messages nevertheless showed longer reaction times to ambiguous than to unambiguous messages. Similarly, Patterson, Cosgrove and O'Brien observed longer reaction times, more hand movements and more eye contact with the speaker when the message was ambiguous rather than unambiguous.

More interestingly, under some conditions children can deliberately make different responses to ambiguous and unambiguous messages. Ackerman reports that when children were lead to mistrust the intention of the speaker, they were more likely to make different responses to ambiguous and unambiguous messages; they were more likely to respond in the same way to the two types of message when they assumed the speaker was telling the truth. Robinson and Whittaker found that children were more likely to respond differently to ambiguous and unambiguous messages when they were prevented from pointing at the potential referents. Instead, they had to tell a puppet which response to make, or they had to post cards with different symbols for ambiguous and unambiguous messages. Normally, and in most of the published studies of children's verbal referential communication skills, children are free to point at the potential referents. Is their knowledge of ambiguity underestimated under these conditions? The results of these studies could be seen as contradictory to our earlier interpretation. We shall discuss this and other possible anomalies later, after we have presented the evidence concerning children's verbal judgements.

Children's judgements of message quality and allocations of responsibility for communicative success or failure

In the judgement tasks we shall summarise in this subsection children are asked to make a verbal judgement, for example: 'Did the speaker do a good job of telling?' or 'Did the speaker say enough for you to get the right one?'. In addition, children might be asked to allocate responsibility for communicative success or failure: e.g. 'Whose fault was it we went wrong?' and 'Why?' The judgements might be made during the course of an exchange in which the children themselves were speakers, or listeners, or observers. Whichever is the case, younger children tend to judge that the speaker did say enough even though the message was ambiguous. Older ones, in contrast, are more likely to judge correctly that the message was inadequate and to specify what was missing from the message. Furthermore, younger children tend to blame listeners for communication failure, on the ground that it was they who went wrong. Older ones tend to blame on the ground that it was they who gave a bad message.

Young children make these incorrect judgements despite:

(1) being capable of making the discriminations and

comparisons necessary for identifying the multiple reference of an ambiguous message, or for identifying the uniquely identifying attributes of one particular referent;

(2) being able to say how many potential referents an ambiguous message has;

(3) saying they are unsure whether their interpretation of an ambiguous message is correct.

It appears then they even if young children have access to the skills and information necessary for identifying ambiguous messages correctly, they still fail to exploit these abilities. Even if they say they are unsure what the speaker means, they still judge that the speaker has told them enough. These children seem simply to be ignorant of the fact that verbal messages can be ambiguous. This conclusion is consistent with certain characteristics of young children's performance as speakers and listeners, as shown in the previous subsection. We shall now consider the performance and judgement data together.

An interpretation of the performance and judgement data

Evidence about children's performance and their judgements in communication tasks suggests the following interpretation: Compared with older children, younger ones do not know that to guarantee successful communication, the speaker must identify the intended referent uniquely from the listener's point of view. Rather, younger children assume that as long as the verbal message is *consistent* rather than inconsistent with the intended meaning, that message is adequate. For example, if the message 'flower' is given to identify a red rather than a blue flower, the message is judged to be adequate.

In contrast, the message 'flag' would be judged to be inadequate by these children.

Neither do younger children maintain a distinction between the speaker's intended meaning on the one hand, and the message used to convey that meaning to a listener on the other. Rather, when the message was in fact ambiguous, they may accept a suggestion that the disambiguated version of the message was actually said.

In contrast, older children's speaking and listening behaviour is more likely to demonstrate that they know how to communicate their intended meanings unambiguously and how to deal effectively with ambiguous messages. Their judgements reveal that they know that for communication to be successful, the speaker's intended meaning must be conveyed unambiguously.

We shall now return to the anomalous performance data presented above: under some conditions children perform as if they do understand about ambiguity. Are we therefore underestimating children's understanding by concentrating on their failures rather than on their successes? This question can be asked about other aspects of children's performance as communicators. For example, under some conditions young children reformulate their messages: they behave as if they know that more information is needed if the listener is to understand the speaker's intended meaning. They will ask disambiguating questions under some conditions.

In each of these three examples, responding differently to ambiguous and unambiguous messages, reformulating an ambiguous message and asking a disambiguating question, children's behaviour is consistent with an understanding of ambiguity. However, in each case children could be making their responses *without* understanding about ambiguity.

First we shall consider the children in the Robinson and Whittaker work mentioned above who responded differently to ambiguous and unambiguous messages only when they could not point at potential referents. These children seemed to be attending to their own uncertainty about the interpretation of ambiguous messages, and basing their correct responses to ambiguous messages on that uncertainty, rather than on a knowledge of ambiguity as such. Children who said they were sure about their interpretation of ambiguous messages responded in the same way to ambiguous and unambiguous messages even when they were prevented from pointing at potential referents.

Secondly, consider the children in the Robinson report who reformulated their ambiguous messages despite giving incorrect judgements of the quality of such messages: they seemed to be using the rule; 'If the listener doesn't respond appropriately, say something else'; they did not without prompting give new information which was useful to the listener.

Finally, the children cited by Robinson and Robinson who asked disambiguating questions despite giving incorrect judgements of the quality of ambiguous messages seemed not to know that more information was *necessary*. They appeared to see question asking as but one way of solving a problem of what to do in response to a message; thinking harder would, they assumed, have been equally effective.

Hence both children's performance as speakers and listeners and their judgements about messages present a consistent picture of their assumptions about the process of verbal communication. Relationships between performance and judgement data provide further support for this interpretation. For certain tasks it can be argued that successful performance *requires* understanding about some feature of the process of communication, and in these cases we have the opportunity to validate our interpretations of children's judgements. For example, children should succeed in deliberately withholding information to make their listener's task difficult only if they understand the significance of unique reference for successful communication. We compared messages given when children were asked deliberately to give ambiguous messages with those given when they were asked to give unambiguous ones. As predicted, only children who made correct judgements of ambiguous messages gave more ambiguous messages under the former conditions than under the latter.

For other tasks, there is no *necessary* relationship between understanding about ambiguity and quality of performance, although one would expect that in general performance should be better among children who understand more about the process of communication. Again, these expectations have been supported. For example, in one task children instructed the experimenter how to build a model out of Lego, and in another how to build a picture out of felt pieces. In both cases, children who correctly judged that their ambiguous instructions had been responsible for the experimenter's errors gave *more* detailed and informative instructions than did children who judged their ambiguous instructions to be adequate. The results were similar when children played in pairs rather than with the experimenter, and when the child listeners were shown how to ask questions when they were unsure what to do.

Young children's implicit assumption is apparently that listeners have at their disposal sufficient information to guarantee a correct interpretation of the speaker's intended meaning, even when the message was in fact ambiguous. This is as expected if children initially treat verbal messages just as they would any other incoming information. Their behaviour is quite consistent with a conception of children who, from earliest infancy, make the best interpretation of incoming information in terms of already developed assumptions of what the world is like, and who change those assumptions only when change is necessary to accommodate new information meaningfully. What we have to explain, then, is how children come to treat verbal messages in a different way, as a 'clue' which may be an ambiguous representation of the speaker's intended meaning. How do children learn that sometimes it is appropriate *not* to make a single interpretation of the incoming information?

Identifying causes of change in understanding about communication

Two sources of information seem to be relevant to an explanation of how children change their conceptions about communication: the results of intervention studies, and naturalistic data. From the first we can draw conclusions about factors which promote change. Analysis of naturalistic data reveals whether those factors occur in children's daily lives. In what follows we consider each of these in turn, and then the relationship between them.

Intervention Studies

A number of recent intervention studies have investigated the conditions under which children's communicative performance and/or their knowledge about communication is improved. For example. Lefebvre-Pinard, Charbonneau and Feider demonstrated improvements in performance resulting from repeatedly asking children to reformulate their messages until they contained only contrasting attributes. Sonnenschein and Whitehurst showed that an effective way of advancing children's performance and judgements was to ask them to evaluate the speaking and listening performance of two dolls.

Another effective intervention technique is to tell children explicitly about the listener's understanding or non understanding. Results of several studies support this suggestion. In these studies children were told during the course of a communication game when and why the listener did or did not understand precisely what the speaker meant. For example, the experimenter might say 'You know which one I mean because there's only one like that' or 'I don't know which one you mean because there are four like that, I need to know some more'. Giving this kind of explicit information resulted in clear advances in children's judgements of ambiguous messages and in their speaking performance. In comparison, if the experimenter guessed what the child meant, or asked questions to elicit information missing from the original message, children did not advance in their judgements or performance.

One possible interpretation of these results is that the children benefited from the information itself. However, the results of further studies suggest that a direct effect of this kind may not have been operating. In one study children were given the explicit information about listener's understanding or non understanding at the end of an exchange. It was relatively ineffective as a means of promoting their understanding about ambiguity and totally ineffective in advancing their performance as listeners or speakers. In this condition children were told, for example, 'I didn't really know which one you meant because there were four like that. I just guessed.' In contrast, in the studies cited above, the explicit information was given during the course of the exchange, immediately following the message. It seems to be under these conditions that explicit information is effective in promoting advances in understanding and in speaking and listening behaviour.

We interpret this finding in the following way. When children are given explicit information during the course of an exchange there are consequences for their listening or speaking behaviour. For example, when the listener says 'I don't know what you mean because there are four like that', the speaker is encouraged to convey the original intended meaning unambiguously. When the speaker says 'You don't know yet which one I mean because there are three red ones', this discourages the listener from making an impulsive interpretation of an ambiguous message. This imposed behaviour is consistent with an accurate conception of communication: the children are encouraged to behave 'as if they already understand about both ambiguity and its role in causing communication failure. It contrasts with the spontaneous behaviour of young children: as listeners they are prepared to interpret ambiguous messages, and as speakers they are prepared to accept interpretations which differ from the original intended meaning. It could be, then, that if children are encouraged to behave in a way which is consistent with an accurate conception of communication, but inconsistent with their current inaccurate one, they somehow come to understand why that new behaviour is appropriate.

This listening and speaking behaviour can be imposed by other means, without telling children explicitly when and why the listener has or has not understood what the speaker meant. For example, the experimenter as listener can refuse to interpret children's ambiguous messages without telling them why, by saying 'I can't really choose yet' and waiting for further clarification. The results of two studies suggest that this latter kind of intervention is almost as effective as is the giving of explicit information during the course of an exchange.

We cannot yet explain precisely how children achieve understanding of ambiguity as a result of imposed changes in their listening and speaking behaviour. Our assumption was that the intervention in some way enabled children to understand the simple fact that verbal messages can be ambiguous. It is possible, however, that it had a more general effect of focusing children's attention on the distinction between the intended meaning and the message itself. We already know that children are often aware of problems with interpretation of ambiguous messages before they come to understand about ambiguity. As mentioned above under 'Age-related Differences in Communicative Performance and in Understanding about Communication', children often say they are unsure whether their interpretation is correct, yet judge that they have been told enough to make the correct interpretation. Once they have been alerted to the meaning-message distinction they have a potential way of making sense of their uncertainty: they are uncertain because the message suggests more than one interpretation of the intended meaning.

How might the intervention have directed children's attention to the distinction between the message and the intended meaning? One distinctive feature was that listeners did not make impulsive interpretations of messages. Whether the children were listeners they were asked 'Can you tell yet?'; on the experimenter's turn, she would announce whether or not she could tell what the speaker meant. This treatment could have encouraged children to treat messages as 'clues' to an intended meaning. Having adopted that approach they may have been able to make the inference that the 'clues' suggest more than one interpretation, and used their uncertainty as a way of identifying such inadequate 'clues'.

Speech to children at home and at school

The above studies demonstrate that under certain conditions we can produce advances in conceptions of communication, with associated advances in performance as listeners and speakers. We now wish to examine how these changes occur in everyday life. If any of the studies is to provide the basis of an explanation of natural development, we must demonstrate that the processes operating in the experiments have parallels in children's everyday lives.

With this aim in mind, we began an analysis of conversation between adults and children in the early school years. The data were collected by other researchers for other purposes: by Clough and by Cambourne in Australia, and by Wells in the UK. Preliminary analyses indicated that some of the processes examined in the successful intervention studies simply did not occur in everyday life. We found no examples of listeners forcing child speakers to reformulate their ambiguous utterances, or of childrer being asked to evaluate the performance of other speakers and listeners. It seems unlikely then that the interventions conducted by Lefebvre-Pinard *et al.* or Sonnenschein and Whitehurst will explain natural development.

In addition, there were few instances of listeners refusing to interpret the child's ambiguous utterances and explaining why interpretation was not possible. In our analyses of Australian and British data we found that at home, at nursery and at infants' school children were hardly ever told explicitly when the listener had not understood what the speaker meant, and were never told why. Nevertheless on the rare occasions when explicit information was given, it was apparently beneficial. In the Robinson and Robinson study we found some mothers who on occasion responded to their children's ambiguous messages by saying 'I don't know what you mean'. They had children who were more advanced in their judgements of ambiguous messages at age 6, than did mothers who took responsibility for solving problems of communication by making guesses or asking questions. It seemed that telling children explicitly that their listener had not understood was an effective way of promoting understanding about communication is real life as well as in experimental settings. In view of the rarity of such occurrences, it is, however, unreasonable to argue that this is the means by which all or even most children come to understand about ambiguity. We need to identify an alternative explanation.

One possible alternative is that suggested by Robinson and Robinson and Robinson and Robinson. On the basis of the intervention studies reported in the previous subsection, we suggested that children may come to understand about ambiguity as a consequence of being induced to behave 'as if they already understand. To find out whether this suggestion had relevance for natural development we examined the Wells naturalistic data for examples of situations in which children were required to behave in this way. We thought, for example, that in school children might be encouraged to generate unambiguous messages by being led to clarify or continue their utterance without explicitly being told why. As speakers they might be expected to wait until a set of instructions was complete before beginning to act upon them. Examination of the data again revealed few instances of either of these phenomena, or of others which could be classified as examples of expecting children to behave as if they understand about ambiguity.

We adopted an alternative research strategy. Instead of examining naturalistic data for parallels with successful experimental interventions, we began our analysis with the naturalistic data in an attempt to identify characteristics of adult-child or child talk which might be relevant to children's learning about the requirements of effective communication. Since this learning seems to take place during the early school years, we searched for potentially relevant characteristics of communication which occurred at that time rather than earlier.

One possibility is that adult-child talk at home changes in significant ways once children go to school and can recount to their parents events of which the parents are genuinely ignorant. Parents may be more concerned than they were previously to understand precisely what their children mean. However, we did not discern any obvious changes in this direction.

A second possibility is that interaction with other children is important for learning the requirements of effective communication. Again, preliminary searches through Cambourne's transcripts of child-child conversation in the playground suggested that this was not a fruitful line to follow since there were very few exchanges of information between the children. Those which did occur rarely lasted more than two turns, and there was very little reformulation by speakers or questioning by listeners.

A third possibility, which is the one we decided to follow up, is that children's talk with teachers has characteristics which are relevant for learning about communication.

We began by identifying ways in which teacher-child talk differed from parent-child talk. We used the data collected by Wells and examined transcripts of the speech of 32 5-year-old children in the classroom and compared this with their speech at home. Our analysis and that conducted by Wells identifies three major differences between adult-child talk in the home and talk at school: the topics of conversation: the giving of instructions; and the sorts of questions asked by adults. We did observe other differences, but it was not clear how these might be related to the changes in which we were interested.

When we compared the topics of conversation at home and at school, we found conversation to be much more adult-centered at school, and more child centered at home. This finding is also reported by Wells in his analyses of the same data. He reports that in school, rather than at home, adults were much more likely to be responsible for initiating conversations, and they were also more likely to extend their own meanings n conversation rather than those of the child. This may be partly responsible for modifying children's conceptions of communication: in adult-centred conversation there may be more adult concern that listener and speaker understand each other, and hence more opportunities for children to realise that communication is at times problematic.

A second difference between home and school was in the frequency with which children received complex instructions. We examined the data for instances in which children were given three or more distinct but consecutive instructions. Overall such extended instructions were much more common in school than at home. Such instructions may encourage children to delay their interpretation of messages. As we have already noted, young children tend to act on ambiguous or incomplete instructions. The extended sequences given at school may discourage children from doing that: it may be that children learn from their initial unsuccessful interpretations following the first instruction of an extended sequence that a better strategy is to delay interpretation until the sequence is complete.

A third way in which conversation differed in the home and at school was in the types of questions asked by adults. Wells found that teachers were much more likely than parents to ask display questions, that is questions to which they already knew the answer, e.g. 'What colour is this?' The use of display questions in school may have implications for learning about communication. Display questions, unlike genuine requests for information, give the speaker, in this case the teacher, the opportunity to assess whether the responder has fully understood the meaning of the message. In such situations, answers are either right or wrong, and as a consequence children may learn that for certain types of messages, specific responses are required and that these are not negotiable.

A final difference between adult-child talk in the home and at school was the occurrence of certain types of sequences of questions at school, which occurred rarely at home. These sequences occurred when teachers were apparently trying to assess the extent of children's understanding or knowledge of some content area. Teachers adopted a technique of asking questions of increased specificity until the children generated the correct answer, or until it became apparent that they were not going to do so, when the teacher would give it herself. Thus, the teacher would begin her assessment by asking a question which was only obliquely related to the topic under discussion. If a correct response was not forthcoming, then she asked a more specific variant of the original question. For example:

Teacher: Why is that on the table?

Children: (No response)

Teacher: Why am I putting these things on this table?

Teacher: What's special about them?

Child: I think all the people like them.

Teacher: All the people like them? What are they all made of?

Child: Wood

How might such sequences contribute to children's learning about communication? One possibility is that they may help children to learn that the intended meaning of a particular message is not always immediately apparent. The experience of attempting to decode the meaning of a teacher's vague questions may bring this home to children. A second way in which children may benefit is that they may learn that a particular intended meaning can be phrased in a number of different ways. This kind of interaction may, then, help children to perfect the distinction between the speaker's intended meaning and the message used to convey that meaning to a listener.

It is interesting to note that other researchers have also isolated some of these differences between talk to children at home and at school, but have seen quite different implications. In particular there has been criticism of the use of display questions by teachers, and also of teachers' failure to expand on the meanings the children themselves express. The claim advanced is that such features of teacher talk stifle children's expression of their ideas and feelings, and additional do not allow children to practise their linguistic skills. While such criticism may be valid,. it is possible that these features may benefit children in other ways. If our speculations about how children learn about communication are correct, then it may be precisely these features of teacher talk which are responsible for those advances. We plan to carry out further work to find out whether our speculations have any validity.

An interpretation of the results of intervention and naturalistic studies.

Our analyses of adult-child talk at home and at school suggest that an explanation of the development of understanding about message ambiguity must attribute a highly active role to the child. Explicit verbal information about communicative success or failure is a relatively rare occurrence. There is also experimental evidence that typical adult behaviour can allow children to assume that listener and speaker understand each other when in fact they do not. It seems, then, that most children have to infer the requirements of effective communication and the causes of communication failure from information which is indirect or even misleading.

Although we have been unable to identify features of adult-child talk which could clearly demonstrate to children that verbal messages can be ambiguous and that ambiguity can cause communication failure, we have suggested that certain characteristics of teacher-child talk might focus children's attention on the meaning-message distinction. Whereas at home children may be free to treat language as transparent, at school they may learn to attend more closely to characteristics of the message itself and to distinguish it more precisely from the speaker's intended meaning. Writers such as Olson and Donaldson have argued that a change of this kind occurs when children go to school, although they have linked it to the beginnings of literacy. There is no inconsistency between the two suggestions, and there may well be a set of experiences to which children are exposed when they go to school, all of which contribute to their perfecting of the distinction between meaning and message.

Conclusions and prospects

Above under the heading 'Age-related Differences in Communicative Performance and in Understanding about Communicative Performance and in Understanding about Communication' we mentioned experimental evidence to support the idea that understanding about ambiguity could be seen as one symptom of having perfected that distinction. The intervention studies summarised above under the heading 'Identifying Cause of Change in Understanding about Communication' can also be interpreted within that broader framework. In our future work we plan to develop and test these interpretations of the intervention and naturalistic data. Clearly there are some circumstances under which young children do distinguish intended meaning from message, as in verbal jokes or in games such as 'I Spy'. In normal conversation, however, they may ignore the distinction. They may be particularly inclined to ignore it when the message suggests at least one clear interpretation, as do the ambiguous messages used in most of the work on verbal referential communication. Are there a number of different ways of focusing children's attention on the meaning-message distinction? Do children encounter these more frequently at school than in the home? Does experience of them lead to advances in understanding about possible causes of communication failure, and if so how? These are some of the questions raised by the work reported in this chapter. It is clear that although we can identify some of the misconceptions young children may have about the process of verbal communication; and can also make recommendations about how to help them achieve a more accurate conception and hereby become more effective communications; we still have much to learn about how they make these advances in their everyday lives.

9

The Emergence of Semantic Relations

The Evidence for combinatorial structure in one-word speech

The results of our study indicate that semantic functions to play a role in the development of one-word speech. An analysis of samples of children's speech recorded at different stages in their development reveals that children are constrained in the number of semantic functions they can express at any given time and that this number changes with time. However, within the confines of these constraints, children use words freely. In other words, semantic functions combine freely with available vocabulary to produce the variety of observed utterances. This combination of constraint and productivity indicates that semantic functions have structural status in one-word speech: Children learning to speak already possess the equivalent of combinatorial rules that can generate a potentially infinite number of situationally distinct messages. In this chapter, we shall first summarize the evidence for such structural status and then discuss the emergence and use of each function in detail.

A limited number of semantic functions

The most general argument for structure in one-word speech follows the lines of McNeill's and Bloom's arguments for the existence of structure in later speech. If there were no structure to single-word utterances, one would not expect to find a constraint in the usage of newly acquired words. Yet, the child clearly is constrained in the combinatorial possibilities of using his lexicon since new words generally take on only a very limited set of usages. For example, at about 14 months of age, Nicky could use a new inanimate-object name to serve only one function—to indicate it. Similarly, before 18 months of age, he could use people's names only to name them, ask for them, or express them as Agents. However, during his nineteenth month, he began to use names in connection with objects associated with a given person. For example, he used *dada* not just to name his father, but also in reference to his father's coat. By the time he was 21 months old, he had extended this new usage to cover most of the names in his vocabulary. A given word can be used in more ways as a child's command of language increases, but there is always a definite limit to the total number of types of uses of a given word. Not just any semantic function appeared in one-word speech, but only the thirteen semantic functions already described. Every one of these functions has its counterpart in later two word speech, where rule-boundedness is not in question.

Developmental sequence

A well-defined developmental sequence is a constraint on random productivity. As Borwn points out, if there were no rules, all possible utterances would appear at once. However, this does not happen, instead, the development follows a generally follows a generally consistent, definite order.

The assessment of order of acquisition is somewhat problematical. How do you know exactly when a child "has" a given semantic function? Although we could use a productivity measure as the criterion for acquisition, this is not entirely satisfactory for several reasons. One is that both boys used many semantic relations before the first formal observation session, and it is difficult to measure productivity from diary observations, our only source of data for this period. A second is that frequency of occurrence, one aspect of productivity is very much affected by situational structure, and some semantic functions are used only in relatively rare situations. Thus, measured productivity is a function of the context and, therefore, does not directly measure children's linguistic abilities. There are a number of semantic functions that occur in single instances during observation sessions well before they achieve productivity.

A third reason is that children's linguistic production is sensitive to the strangeness of the environment, so the strangeness of an observation session inhibits a child's use of newly acquired relations. For example, Matthew's first Indicative Object is reported in his diary at 8, yet no reliable spontaneous instance occurred in a formal session until Matthew II-14.

Although the diary observations offer no quantitative measure of productivity, they are much better suited to catching the rarer types of utterance. This is shown by the fact that all of Matthew's semantic functions and all except two of Nicky's were noted first in the diaries. For this reason, we decided to use the first recorded example of each semantic function to establish and compare orders of development for the two boys. This method allows us to include data from both diary and formal observation.

Even though single examples can the flukes, as Brown has pointed out, the first recorded appearance does seem more likely to get at underlying capacity or competence than does a quantitative measure. All of the relations that were recorded in diaries also occurred during a formal session from a few days to a few months later. This pattern confirms the usefulness and reliability of diary data for the study of early speech.

Table 1

Onset.of semantic functions: Order and first occurance for Nicky

Semantic function	Age	Instance
Performative	8(19)	*dada*, to accompany every action
Performative Object	9(8)	*dada*, looking at father
Volition	11(28)	*na, na,* Crawing to forbidden bookcase
Agent	13(3)	*dada,* hearing someone come in
Action or State of Agent	14 (21)-15(18)	*do(wn)*, when he sits or steps down
Object	16(19-25)	*bar* (fan), demanding fan to be turned on or off
Dative	18 (4)[b]	*mama,* when he gives look to mother
Object Associated with Another object of location	18(8-16)	*poo*, putting his hand on bottom while being changed, usually after a bowd movement
Animate being associated	18(19-25)	*lara*(Lauren) upon seeing her empty bed
with object for location	18 (19-25)	*bap* (diaper) to indicate location of fees
Modification of event	19(29)[b]	*more record*, pointig to record playing

Tables 1 and 2 show the ages at which different semantic

functions first occurred in diary and formal-session data for both boys, and describe the first recorded example of each function. The development within each function after its first appearance will be examined in the sections that follow. In comparing the development of the two boys, sequence is much more important than age. Thus, we do not compare the age of acquisition of a given function, but compare its position in the developmental sequences. Such emphasis on sequence and de-emphasis of chronological age is consistent with current thinking in developmental psychology.

Table 2

Onset of semantic function: order and first occurrence for Matthew

Semantic function	*Age*	*Instance*
Performative	7(22)	*hi,* as accompaniment to waving
Performative Object	8(12)	*dada,* looking at father
Volition	11(24)	*nana,* turning away from stairs in response to mother's no[a]
Dative	11(28)	*dada,* offering bottle to father
Object	13(0)	*ba(ll),* having just thrown ball
Agent	13(3)	*daddy,* hearing father come in door and start up steps
Action or state of Agent	13(16)	up, reaching up, in answer to question *Do you want to get up?*[a]
Action or State of Object	14(6)	*down,* having just thrown something down
Object Associated with Another Object or Location	14(29)	*caca* (cracker, cookie), pointing to door to next room, where cookies are kept
Location	15(20)	*bo(x),* putting crayon in box
Animate Being Associated with Object or Location	15(29)	*fishy,* pointing to empty fish tank
Modification of Event	ca 18(1)	*Again,* when he wants someone to do something for him again

The order of appearance of the different functions is substantially similar for the two boys. The Kendall rank order correlation between the order of first appearance of each semantic appearance of each semantic function for the two boys is .83 significant at the .0001 level. It is possible that the true correlation could be even higher, since the largest reduction results from a diary example involving an ambiguous vocabulary item. This is Matthew's first expression of Dative, when he hands his father a bottle while saying *dada*, at 11. Earlier, he had been using a similar syllable, *dat,* as a Performative to accompany many actions; it is difficult to distinguish the two usages in this example.

If we segregate the functions into the larger categories indicated by the groupings in the tables, the agreement of orders of appearance is perfect. The order is: performative functions, functions involving a relation between an entity and an action, relations between two entities, and modification of events.

The similarity of the developmental sequences of the two boys cannot be attributed to the influence of expectations, as Nicky's mother was not aware of any hypotheses about order of development. The parallel development of semantic functions in the two boys reflects a parallel sequence of semantic interpretation in the two mothers, and thus constitutes evidence that one-word utterances are, in fact, systematic in their communicative effect. These results militate against the idea that early language, being egocentric, fails to communicate.

This developmental sequence also belies the idea that the first use of language is to express orders and desires. Performatives certainly do not express desire, although they may not be language either. If one considers that Performative Objects are the first example of language proper, it is clear from Tables 1 and 2 that the first instances are Indicative rather than Volitional. Volitional Objects occur later for both boys. The first example of a Volitional Object noted for Matthew occurs at 9(16), when he says *mamama*, gesturing that he wants mother 1 month after the first instance of naming an Indicative Object. For Nicky, the first clear-cut example occurs between 14(12 and 14(18) when he says *Do(t)?*, looking for her. The expression of Volition itself occurs after the first Indicative Objects, as Tables 1 and 2 show.

The sequence shown in Tables 1 and 2 agrees with the less detailed sequence noted by Werner and Kaplan. "Identifying predications," the first stage in Werner and Kaplan's scheme, corresponds to our Indicative type of Performative Object. "Predications of action," the second stage in their scheme, corresponds to our two Action or State categories. "Predications of attribution," their third stage, corresponds to our two categories that involve association. In fact, Werner and Kaplan present an example of a "Predication of attribution" that is almost identical to Nicky's first expression of Object Associated with Another Object or Location, shown in Table 1.

Tables 1 and 2 also show that every semantic function made its first appearance in single-word form, except Nicky's Modification of Event, the last function to develop. Nicky's Modification of Event, the one seeming exception, is not actually inconsistent, for it appears *after* Nicky has used two-word utterances in a formal session.

Productive of semantic functions

To demonstrate that the semantic functions we have

defined have structural status in early speech, it is desirable to show that they all are used productively. This can be done by measuring the variety and frequency of their use during the observation sessions. Tables 3 and 4 show the number of examples of each semantic function in isolated one-word utterances produced during each formal observation period. Because examples with insufficient contextual information could not be interpreted reliably and because multimorpheme single-word utterances were counted. Within a session, instances of a given relation are broken down according to whether they are unique examples or identical to some other utterance during that session. During a session, if a child used the same word in the same way, combined with the same general contextual elements, more than once, then only one such instance was added to the first figure for that session; the remainder were added to the second figure. The first figure thus represents the combinatorial productivity of a particular semantic function at a particular period.

If we define the achievement of productivity by a function as the occurrence of three nonrepetive instances during a single session, then all but three functions achieved productivity in the speech of both boys during the observation period. Modification of an Event was never used extensively by Nicky. Performatives were never recorded in great number for Matthew; Animate Beings Associated with an Object or Location were also rare for Matthew. During the last observation period, the productivity of one-word semantic functions declines, as functions originally expressed by means of a single word gain expression in multiword sentences.

Productivity of individual words and gestures within a single semantic relation

The productivity of child language can perhaps be appreciated better by considering how a given word can be used in a variety of situations while the semantic function remains constant. This phenomenon was noted by Guillaume. During VI—18(18), Matthew used *gone* in relation to six different inanimate objects—everything from juice, to pieces missing from a toy, to an airplane. Illustrations of the various combinations are presented in Table 5. Within the confines of a given relation, Action or State of an Object, this word achieves great productivity through combination with varying but appropriate situational elements.

Like individual words, individual gestures and actions have a generative or productive aspect. For example, the pointing gesture functions as an indicator. Each child could point to and name a seemingly unlimited number of objects. Performative gestures, like reaching or pointing, become virtually as conventionalized as words and, undoubtedly, combine with more situational and verbal elements than any single word.

Single Word, Multiple Functions:

Semantic Development in Individual Vocabulary

As a final illustration of productivity at the one word stage, we shall give some examples of the use of a single word in several semantic functions. One such example was Matthew's us of *yaya*, presented in Section 2.4. As a second example, consider his use of *dada.* Here, we give the earliest recorded instances of its use in different functions.

Table 3

Frequency of semantic functions expressed as isolated single-word utterances at different periods in Nicky's development

Semantic function	Period I 18(4)			Period II 18(27)			Period III 19(29)			Period IV 20(23)		
	Dif.	Same	Total	Dif.	Same	Total	Dif.	Same	Total	Dif.	Same	Total
Performative	2	5	7	1	5	6	3	1	4	1	-	1
Object of Performative Action Indication	10	-	10	37	11	48	18	-	18	25	3	28
Volition	22	1	23	3	-	3	3	-	3	2	-	2
Object of Performative Action	4	-	4	3	-	3	7	-	7	5	1	6
Agent	1	-	1	1	-	1	1	-	1	1	-	1
Action or State of Agent	2	-	2	7	11	18	6	-	6	3	-	3
Object	2	-	2	8	2	10	14	-	14	9	-	9
Action or State of Object	-	-	0	8	5	13	10	-	10	16	1	17
Dative	2	-	2	-	-	0	4	-	4	3	-	3
Object Associated with Another Object or Location	-	-	0	2	-	2	11	-	11	4	1	5
Animate Being Associated with Object or Location	-	-	0	2	-	2	1	-	1	7	-	7
Location	-	-	0	-	-	0	-	-	0	1	-	1
Modification of Event	-	-	0	-	-	0	-	-	0	-	-	0

Table 3(Contd.)

Frequency of semantic functions expressed as isolated single-word utterances at different periods in Nicky's development

	Period V		*21(17)*	*Period VI*		*22(21)*	*Period VII*		*23(21)*	*Period VIII*		*24(23)*
Semantic function	*Dif.*	*Same*	*Total*	*Dif.*	*Same*	*Total*	*Dif.*	*Same*	*Total*	*Dif.*	*Same*	*Total*
Performative	3	-	3	-	-	0	1	-	1	3		3
Object of Performative Action Indication	21	4	25	27	1	28	20	1	21	16	-	16
Volition	10	-	10	2	-	2	3	-	3	2	-	2
Object of Performative Action	7	-	7	5	-	5	10	-	10	5	-	5
Agent	1	-	1	4	-	4	3	-	3	-	-	0
Action or State of Agent	8	2	10	23	2	25	13	-	13	3	-	3
Object	14	-	14	28	1	29	28	-	28	5	-	5
Action or State of Object	24	1	25	28	4	32	22	-	22	5	-	5
Dative	3	1	4	6	-	6	1	-	1	-	-	0
Object Associated with Another Object or Location	1	-	1	8	1	9	3	-	3	1	-	1
Animate Being Associated with Object or Location	1	-	1	1	-	1	3	-	3	2	-	2
Location	6	1	7	2	-	2	1	-	1	-	-	0
Modification of Event	-	-	0	1	-	1	1	-	1	2	-	2

Table 4 Frequency of semantic functions expressed as isolated single-word utterances at different periods in Matthew's development

	Period I 12(15) 12(22)			Period II 14(10) 14(18)			Period III 15(5) 15(17)			Period IV 16(2)			Period V 17(3)		
Semantic function	Dif.	Same	Total	Dif.	Same	Total	Dif.	Same	Total	Dif.	Same	Total	Dif.	Same	Total
Performative	-	-	0	1	-	1	1	-	1	1	-	1	1	-	1
Objective of Performative Action: Indication	-	-	0	10	-	10	13	1	14	9	-	9	3	-	3
Volition	8	-	8	-	-	0	10	-	10	-	-	0	9	-	9
Object of Performative Action: Volition	2	-	2	-	-	0	8	1	9	4	-	4	18	1	19
Agent	-	-	0	-	-	0	-	-	0	-	-	0	-	-	0
Action or State of Agent	-	-	0	4	1	5	12	2	14	18	2	20	16	1	17
Object	-	-	0	2	-	2	5	-	5	18	1	19	5	-	5
Action or state of Object	-	-	0	1	-	1	-	-	0	7	-	7	6	-	6
Dative	-	-	0	-	-	0	-	-	0	1	-	1	-		1
Object Associated with another Object or Location	-	-	0	-	-	0	4	-	4	6	-	6	3	-	3
Animate Being Associated with Object or Location	-	-	0	-	-	0	-	-	0	1	-	1	1	-	1
Location	-	-	0	-	-	0	-	-	0	-	-	0	-	-	0
Modification of Event	-	-	0	-	-	0	-	-	0	-	-	0	-	-	0

Semantic function	Period VI		18(18)	Period VII		19(21)	Period VIII		20(26)	Period IX		22(1)
	Dif.	*Same*	*Total*	*Dif.*	*Same*	*Total*	*Dif.*	*Same*	*Total*	*Dif.*	*Same*	*Total*
Performative	1	-	1	-	-	0	-	-	0	-	-	0
Object of Performative Action: Indication	16	2	18	10	-	10	7	-	7	9	-	9
Volition	7	-	7	10	-	10	15	-	15	3	-	3
Object of performative Action: Volition	5	-	5	11	-	11	8	1	9	2	-	2
Agent	-	-	0	3	-	3	3	-	3	-	-	0
Action or State of Agent	19	-	19	11	1	12	23	4	27	11	1	12
Object	5	-	5	14	1	15	6	-	6	1	-	1
Action or State of Object	21	-	21	16	2	18	17	-	17	6	1	7
Dative	-	-	0	2	-	2	3	1	4	-	-	0
Object Associated with Another object or Location	1	-	1	2	-	2	-	-	0	-	-	0
Animate Being Associated with Objective or Location	2	-	2	-	-	0	2	-	2	2	-	2
Location	-	-	0	2	-	2	4	-	4	1	-	1
Modification of Event	2	-	2	3	-	3	5	-	5	3	-	3

At 8(12), Matthew says *dada* while looking at his father. Here, *dada* is an Indicative Object. At 11(28), he says *dada* while offering a bottle to his father. *Dada* is a Dative in this situation. At 13(3), he says *daddy* upon hearing his father come in the door and start up the steps. *Daddy* is an agent in this context. At 17(15), Matthew says *daddy,* pointing to a cup that belongs to his father. *Daddy* here represents an Animate Being Associated with an Object or Location. At 18(11), *daddy* functions as an Agent in response to the question, *Who went bye-bye?* Whereas Matthew previously had expressed Agents in reaction to perceived events, here, he is responding to a verbaly presented situation. The event is brought to his attention by the question *Who went bye-bye*? This example illustrates another developmental theme of our findings: In general, each function first appears in relation to perceived situational elements, and only later in relation to a linguistic representation of those elements.

At 20(3), Matthew uses *daddy* in a Comitative sense in reply to the question: *Do you want to go with mommy?* The Comitative is tentatively proposed by Fill more as the conjunction of two nouns, often signaled by the preposition *with.* It intrinsically involves a sequence of at least two nouns and so was not treated as a separate semantic function in our analysis of one-word utterances. In this example, *daddy* implicitly replaces *mommy* as object of the preposition *with,* and thus constitutes an example of paradigmatic substitution.

That same day, Matthew's father asks the question *who am I?* and Matthew answers *dady*. Here, an early semantic function, Indicative Object, is expressed in relation to a *wh* question, implicitly filing the shot occupied by *Who* in the question. Thus, Matthew's word for father, the first adult word he acquires, is used successively in all semantic functions which an animate noun an fulfill.

As a third example, consider Matthew's consider Matthew's use of *bye-bye*, an early relational word. *Bye-bye* is initially, at 13(26), a Performative, functioning as the verbal aspect of the act of waving. However, at 14(3), Matthew progresses to using *bye-bye* to represent his own Action or State of motion, saying *bye-bye* while riding his bike, for instance. At 14(29), he uses *bye-bye* while playing with his toy cars, thus encoding the Action or State of an Object. Not until 16(2) does Matthew use *bye-bye* to express the Action of an Agent other than himself: He says bye-bye to report that a visitor is about to leave. This example illustrates the more general developmental finding that children encode their *own* actions or states before the actions or states of *others*. The development of *bye-bye* again shows that new uses become possible for an old word as semantic development proceeds.

These examples show that the range of possible uses of a word at a given stage of a child's development is not solely dependent on the referential meaning of that word. Rather, it also depends on the semantic functions the child can express at that time. Thus, old vocabulary items are used in new ways as semantic development proceeds. The limited range of early speech is not merely a result of limited vocabulary; limitations on the number of semantic relations are just as important.

Developmental change in the expression of semantic relations: An overview

In what follows, we shall give a more detailed picture of semantic relations from a developmental perspective,

Table 5 Action or state of inanimate object: examples of single-word utterances involving gone at Mathew VI-18(18)

Preceding context		Modality			Event	
	M	looking into		container	empty	of juice
					gone	
Milk carton has been empty (unaware now full)	M	pointing to		mild carton	*gone*	
				M	Has taken off rings from toy	
					gone	
	M	looking at			empty	record jacket
					gone, gone, gone	
Gone, yeah,					*record*	
Where's the record? gone						
Gone.					*no*	
					all gone	
All gone? You know Where						
The record is. It's up there.					*gone*	
It's gone cause it's up there.						
It's going round and round.						
The record's going round and round.					*gone*	
It's not gone, It's here.						
Look. Here's the record.					*gone*	
What is it?	M	looking	for spot of light		going around	on ceiling
					round-n-round	
Huh?					*round-n-round*	
					round-n-round	

emphasizing regularities, but noting some differencies in the development of the two boys. Their development will be delineated with respect to a number of different aspects including the relevant situational cues and their structure.

First, we shall watch the development of the child's ability to use each semantic function in combination with verbal as well as situational context. Children usually begin using a semantic function in isolated words and only later use that same function in single-word answers to questions and retorts to statements.

Second, we shall trace the development of the expression of each semantic relation from expression in single words, through expression in multiword sequences, to expression in two-word form. The differences between these types of utterances were noted in section 2.2. The role of verbal context in this progression will be observed. In particular, sequences with intervening adult responses—conversational sequences—will be distinguished from simple sequences.

Third, we shall look at the content of the utterances involving each semantic function in terms of the child's involvement in the situation to which his single word makes reference. We shall examine the evidence for a decentration process in which the child becomes increasingly able to encode events external to himself.

Finally, we shall attempt to analyze the development of the range of expression of each semantic function, insofar as it is distinct from the other progressions we have noted.

The plan of the rest of the chapter is as follows: Semantic functions will be taken up one at a time in the order of their appearance in Nicky's speech. A short introduction to the nature of each function is given. In the section covering each semantic function, its development will be traced chronologically from its appearance in single-word form to its use in two-word sentences. Generally, Nicky's development is discussed first, and Matthew's is compared to it. A summary of their development is provided at the end of each section. Examples are selected to show the earliest instance of each function and other occurrences of interest. All of the first occurrences and many of the other examples are listed in Tables at the end of this chapter, to allow the reader to compare development across functions. Tables 3 through 4 should also help the reader coordinate the development of different functions within a single temporal framework. The summaries at the end of each section and at the end of the chapter allow a general overview of Matthew and Nicky's development. Tables in the text present a representative sampling of different functions and forms. Because the focus of this study was one-word speech, examples of longer utterances are generally given only to illustrate the transition to more mature forms.

Performatives

Both children began speaking by using nonstandard sounds to accompany their actions. Later, they used easily recognizable words in similar ways. Some words are used first in a Performative sense and are later transferred to factual statements. This developmental sequence was noted by Gregoire, who observed a child in whom the first significant word started out as a train sound. The connection with action is less strong in later usage, but Performatives retain the characteristic of constituting an act.

Nicky

The first speech sounds Nicky used consistently were a nonreferential *dada,* 8(19), to accompany many actions for a period. Around 12(7), his mother report that he says *ada* and similar sounds while pointing to things around the house "meaning a sort of 'eureka/there it is.' Does not appear to be attempting to communicate anything to anyone." The following week she writes, "N. points to things with one of the 'words' above—but predominantly *ada* and seems to *expect* to be told the name. He then repeats the *intonation* of the name with one of the 'words' above." The first reported example of a Performative with a conventional word is at 13(8) when Nicky began to say *hi*! to other people. At 13(18), he waved and said *bye-bye* to say good night to his father. The following day, he repeated this when his father left for work. He had known how to wave for at least a month. Later, he learned to use *bye-bye* without the accompanying wave, thereby substituting the word for the action. Table 6 presents a sample of Performatives from Nicky's observation sessions. Since Performatives, by their nature, often are used in imitative responses, imitated words have been included in the frequency count.

Matthew

Matthew's use of Performatives is analogous to Nicky's. From 7(22), he used *ah* (hi) to accompany a wave. At 8(6), he said *dat* to accompany clapping and while playing pat-a-cake. During the same period, he smiles and says *mm* while eating a cracker. Table 2 shows few cases of Performatives of Matthew because most of the examples were imitative and hence eliminated from the analysis. Table 7 includes imitations in the frequency count and presents some examples from Matthew's observation sessions.

Table 6 Frequency and examples of performatives at different periods in Nicky's Development

Observation Period	and age	Frequency	Examples		
			Preceding context	Modality	Event
I	*18(4)*	*8*	*Bye bye bye*	N going to	bed
II	18(27)	6		N finishes tower *(hurr)ay*	
III	19(29)	4		repeats *hurray*	N puts together two balls of play dough
IV	20 (23)	2	camera is on. Say "hi"	N pointing to *hi*	camera
V	21(17)	4		N clapping *hurray*	
VI	22(21)	1	*Nightnight*, Nicky.	*night night*	
VII	23(21)	1	Mother singing song; about to sing "baby."	*baby*	
VIII	24(23)	3		N goes over to repeats *hi*	Lauren

Table 7. Frequency and examples of performatives at different periods in Matthew's Development

Observation Period	and age	Frequency	Examples: Preceding context	Modality	Event
I	12(15) 12(22)	0			
II	14(10) 14(18)	1		M points to and tries to pick up *hi*	picture of telephone receiver
III	15(5) 15(17)	1		M waving out the window *bye*	
IV	16(2)	2	Bernice has entered the car.	M *hi*	
V	17(13)	4	*say "bye"*	M talking into telephone *bye*	
VI	18(18)	4	M has put all the rigs on his toy.	M *yay*	
VII	19(21)	1	*Can you say "bye?"*	*bye*	

Conclusion

The earliest Performatives are on the borderline of language proper. These examples lack complete separation of word and referent and are part of the child's own nonverbal action. With development, more language-like forms appear. This forms are more decentered and less tied to the child's own action: The word substitutes for an action rather than merely accompanying it. For example, the greeting *hi* is first part of the act of waving; later it functions as a greeting without a wave. This separation from the child's own actions is a form of decentration; egocentric speech is clearly not the "all-or-nothing" matter implied by Piaget.

Indicative objects

A child's next messages call attention to objects by naming them—the first instance of language proper. This order appears to be confirmed by the observations of Leopold and others.

Nicky

Nicky used *dada* at 9(8). Like Matthew, he was taught the meaning of *dada* as soon as he started focusing on this double syllable in his babbling, as part of a replication of another study. *Mama* was first observed as an Indicative Object for Nicky at 12(7).

Whereas the performative modality elements is implicit in the child's directed visual attention in these earliest instances of naming, it takes on the more explicit form of pointing as development proceeds. The indicative gesture of pointing is not joined with real naming in its developmental beginnings starting at 12(7). Nicky goes around the house saying different double syllables while pointing to various objects. These syllables have no stable referents, and therefore cannot be considered words, but the context shows clearly that their function is to call attention to objects. Nicky first labels an inanimate object, *ba(ll),* at 13(9). In this example, Nicky says the name while looking at the referent. Later, pointing becomes joined with the stable names that are developing at the same time.

Although Nicky names animate entities before inanimate, he names himself relatively late. Between 20(3) and 20(10), Nicky touches his head and says *nini*, the first instance of self-indication. This accomplishment would seem to indicate decentration from an earlier stage in which the child took himself for granted and was unaware of himself as an entity to be named.

Sometime after being able to name Objects of Indicative Action, Nicky can answer *wh* questions. During Nicky I—18(4), he responds to the question *What is that?* by pointing and saying *baby*. Nicky would not, of course, have to understand the full question in order to respond, since comprehension of question intonation and the mother's pointing gesture would suffice to give a response. Indeed, it is probably the rule that adult verbal context is *added* to, and is not a substitute for gesture and other nonverbal elements in early dialogue. The fact that Nicky used the word *dat* in his own pointing messages during the same session, shows that he could understand the word *that* in the question. Nicky's pointing gesture provides supporting evidence that he really is responding to the question. *Baby* may therefore be considered to fit into the structural framework provided by the question, and thus implies the message *That is baby*. Because both the demonstrative and the specific name refer to an entity that is the object of pointing, these two types are placed in the same semantic category. Implicit in this is the recognition that object existence and object place are not linguistically differentiated at this stage, for pointing simultaneously indicates both the location and the existence of something. The common origin of existence and location in pointing is consist with—and, in an onto genetic sense, perhaps explains—the fact that existential and locative constructions are closely related from a formal, linguistic point of view and have a common locative basis in many languages.

Sequences involving indication occur from Nicky I—18(4), where, for instance, he says *mommy; dat,* pointing to a picture. At Nicky IV—20(23), there is a conversational sequence in which Nicky names and Indicative Object, is corrected by his mother, and then imitates her correction.

The sequence looks very much like a situational analog to a paradigmatic word association, in which words filling the same syntactic function are associated. It contrasts with earlier sequences, analogous to syntagmatic associations, in which words filling complementary but dissimilar functions are uttered in sequence. An example of the latter type of sequence occurred at Nicky I—18(4), when Nicky said *mommy* followed by *dat* while pointing to a picture. Here, *dat* is an Indicative Object, while *mommy* is a vocative. Thus, syntagmatic sequences precede paradigmatic ones, just as syntagmatic word associations precede paradigmatic ones. These list like paradigmatic sequences continue in Nicky's later speech.

Indication assumes multiword form for the first time at Nicky VIII—24(23). In asking the question *Who dat?,* he differentiates between object and name. During the same session, he explicitly differentiates between Object and Location in the three-word utterance *here* it is, which he says when he finds a number 6 under a lid. Whereas the act of pointing can refer to either an object or a place, in this sentence, *here* can refer only to the Location.

Negative Indication

One particular type of indication, the negative, must be treated separately. Although we originally treated negation as a single category, it was semantically diverse and, unlike our other categories, was defined in terms of lexical items. Consequently, we decided to categorize *no* according to the semantic scope of its negation. Of the early students of one-word speech, Gregoire was particularly astute in noting the semantic diversity single-word negation; he contrasts refusal with nonexistence, absence, or disappearance.

Negative Indication makes its first appearance at Nicky II—18(27) when Nicky says *no; no,* referring to the fact that there is no milk in a cup. This type of Negative Indication corresponds to Bloom's category of nonexistence. Negation was the one area in which Bloom was willing to assign semantic structure to single word utterances; she, too, found examples of nonexistence expressed in single-word form. Nonexistence develops into two-word form in the next formal session, Nicky III—19(29): Nicky, who has been crying, says *no daddy* when his father is not at home.

A second type of Negative Indication is an instance of what Bloom term denial and the McNeills call negation of truth: An object name is denied. It makes its first appearance at Nicky III when Nicky draws a picture of something that is not an eye and says *no eye.* Other examples of these two types of negative Indication occur in later sessions. It is interesting that the first two word utterance expressing denial occurs at the same time as the fist two-word utterance expressing nonexistence, although the latter had earlier been expressed in single-word form. Negative Volition and denial of an Action or State will be taken up later when the corresponding semantic functions are presented.

Matthew

Matthew's development of naming parallels Nicky's Matthew used *dada* looking at his father at 1(12), he began to use the same double syllable *dada* for doggie, probably because of his limited phonological system. At 8(30), Matthew answered his first *wh* question: His mother said *Who's that?*, pointing to a picture of a dog, and he answered *da*. Thus, expression of the Object of Indicative Action occurs later developmentally in relation to verbal context than in relation to situational context alone.

Like Nicky, Matthew does not point at what he names until later. The first instance recorded in his diary is at 10(9), pointing to a dog going down the street. Matthew named the Object of this Indicative Action twice during the first formal observation period—his eye once and a bird once. In both cases, the label was instigated by his mother's mention of the word. Therefore, they were omitted from the productivity table even though each label was accompanied by an appropriate pointing gesture.

During the second observation period, at 14(10, 18), this semantic function achieves true productivity; there are 10 reliable occurrences with 5 different words. On four of these occasions, the name is a response to the questions

What is that? In 9 of 10 cases, naming is accompanied by pointing: thus, pointing is very much a part of this semantic function at the time it first achieves productivity. The constant relation between naming and pointing at this stage suggests that the gesture is a fundamental aspect of the semantic structure. In other words, the performative element, in this case the Indicative gesture of pointing, is not just an incidental characteristic of early speech. In Matthew's later observation periods naming gradually is freed from the act of pointing, just as it was for Nicky. At Matthew VI—18(18), the point at which Objects of Indicative Action reach their highest frequency, Matthew reliably names 6 different objects a total of 7 times while pointing at them, and 8 objects, a total of 11 times in combination with other Performative gestures like holding or looking at the named object. Where naming is accompanied by looking at the object named, the Performative element is, again, becoming relatively internal and implicit. The important developmental trend, however, is the diversification of Indicative Actions—the relative independence of naming from pointing in comparison with Matthew II, when this semantic function first became productive.

One type of name is somewhat problematical. Both Matthew and Nicky used animal sounds alternatively to name an animal and to describe what it does. Thus, if a child look at a dog and says *woof woof,* his mother's reply might be either *Yes, that's a doggie,* or *Yes, a doggie goes woof woof.* If the child did not have another name for the animal, the animal was silent, and the child used a clear Indicative gesture, then the occurrence was counted as an Object of Indicative Action. If, on the other hand, the animal was in the process of making sounds or sounds were implied by the previous question, then the utterance was classified as Action or State of Agent. Many instances of animal sounds, however, lacked these criteria, were considered ambiguous, and were therefore excluded from the reliable utterances tabulated in Tables 10 and 11. The use of animal sounds to name an animal is hard to evaluate; it may, in fact, be nothing more than an early form of onomatopoeia.

Unlike Nicky, Matthew often uses *yeah* to express assent or agreement. The earliest instances in connection with naming occur at Matthew VI—18(18):

Mother	Matthew
That's Bernice]s pen.	*Yeach*

Although interesting, *yeah* is ambiguous because it is impossible to know whether *yeah* affirms the identity of the pen or its possession by Bernice. Perhaps, however, additional situational information could clarify the scope of the affirmation in this type of situation. For example, if Matthew had been playing with the pen and his mother had asked him to stop, then we might infer that the pen's identity was presupposed and that Bernice's ownership was what was affirmed. On the other hand, if Matthew's mother had just pointed out Bernice's pencil, then we might infer that the object's identity as a pen was the affirmed relation.

Like Nicky, Matthew expresses negative Indication, although less frequently. An example involving a conversational sequence occurs at Matthew VIII—20(26):

Mother	Matthew
	(My points to bear)

	giraffe
Is that a giraffe	*no*
What is it?	*bear*

One example of nonimitated negative indication in two-word form occurs for Matthew during the period under study. During the same session, Matthew's mother asks *Do you want to put the duck in?*, referring to an inlaid puzzle. Matthew puts the duck piece in the tree hold and says no *no tree,* apparently denying that it is a tree. Corresponding to Matthew's use of *yeah* in isolated single-word utterances to affirm the identity of something is his use of *yeah* in indicative sequences. The first example occurs at Matthew VIII-20(26):

The example also shows how, once Matthew acquires the affirmative word *yeah,* his mother uses it to check her interpretations of his speech. Such verbal confirmations of semantic interpretations are another piece of evidence in favor of correspondence between the basic semantic structure of child utterance and adult interpretation.Like Nicky, Matthew forms sequences involving Objects of Indicative Action. The earliest example, at Matthew II—14(10, 18), is one in which Matthew names something, is corrected by his mother, and then imitates the correction:

Mother	Matthew
	(Matthew picks up) pot piece of puzzle)
What is that?	*pot*
Is that a pot?	*Yeah*

At Matthew III-15(5, 17), Indicative Objects occur in repetitive sequence in which Matthew repeats the same word at different points in the conversation. For example:

Mother	Matthew
	(Matthew looking at picture of door)
	door
	(Matthew pointing to picture of door)
Where's the door	*door*

The significance of this sort of sequence seems to be that it provides an opportunity for repetitive practice and for the clarification of messages. Although repetitive sequences occur for a variety of semantic functions, they will not be mentioned in later sections because they appeared to be of less theoretical significance than nonrepetitive sequences.

Like Nicky, Matthew forms sequences in which an Indicative relation embeds another semantic relation as the sequence progresses. The earliest example is at Matthew V—17(13). When Matthew says *nany*, his mother answers *What?*, and he responds *lara*. His mother then queries *Does Lauren have candy?* and he nods affirmatively. *Navy* at first appears to be simply a name, but then turns out also to be something associated with his sister Lauren.

De Laguna and Werner and Kaplan among others have written of a developmental transition in which the pointing gesture is augmented or replaced by a demonstrative form to yield a two-word utterance like "this X." Brown refers to two-word identifications like "this X" as Nomination, and notes the universality of this operation of reference. As in the case of Nicky, two-word utterances of this sort develop late in the period under consideration, during Matthew's last three observation periods. An example from Matthew IX—22(1) occurs when Matthew picks up his sock and says *this one*.

For both Matthew and Nicky, language proper begins by naming Indicative Objects. This developmental priority of Indication in the case of both boys constitutes counter evidence to the claim of Piaget, Jakobson, and others that the first use of language is to express orders and desire. From both a logical and psychological point of view, naming entities is basic to all semantic relations in which an entity is expressed. Once able to express Indicative Objects, the child has made the basic leap to language proper. He now has points of reference for the language—world correspondence.

Both children name people—animate objects—before inanimate objects, and name themselves only much later. The behavioral manifestation of Indication shows a developmental shift from looking to a pointing gesture to free use of a variety of means of Indication.

Pointing utterances differ from what we have termed "pure" Performatives in that pointing is the gestural representation of the Indicative Mode. Pointing can thus be considered the action translation of the semantic class of indicative verbs such as *show* and *indicate*, which Austin and Ross treated in their discussion of Performatives. Like linguistic Performatives, the pointing gesture takes a complement, in this case an entity; and the entity is encoded verbally with a label as well. Thus, pointing at something that is named constitutes a synthesis of two earlier developments—the "pure" Performative on the borderline of language proper, and the name. Hence, the Performative becomes part of the contextual framework, enacted by child and interpreted by adult, but is not given linguistic expression. the pointing gesture itself achieves productivity, for it becomes capable of being combined with an infinite number of objects.

Whereas, initially, the children use names only in response to objects themselves, they later do so in response to verbal context and questions such as *What's that?* Later developments of Indication include equative statements, such as *this bear,* and question, such as *who dat?* Children also encode their own Indication with verbs such as *touch* and *have;* however, these utterances could be considered as constative rather than performative. Negative statements of non-existence and denial are made relatively late.

Naming is the basis for subsequence language use. Thus Indicatives come to be incorporated into sequences and embedded within other functions.

Volition

Volitional utterances appear only after the Indicative is established. With the appearance of these utterances, the child has two modes the Indicative and the Volitional at his disposal. The two modes are generally differentiated by intonation or gesture. This contrast between Indication and Volition corresponds to Lewis' distinction between the declarative and manipulative functions of early words, the former used to draw attention, the latter to demand. It similarly corresponds to Leopold's distinction between statements of fact and emotional utterances. Because the children had three main words to express volition—*mama, no,* and *yes*—this section, unlike the others, will be organized mainly in terms of specific lexical items. All three words were used in other semantic functions as well; the present section deals only with their use in Volition.

Mama

Mama is probably the single most confusing word that children use. It is often their first linguistic means for expression desire or volition. *Mama* probably derives from the "call sounds" that Werner and Kaplan and others have noted in connection with staining movements of the child toward objects. They point out that because the child is directing itself toward a distant object while making them, call sounds are a step in the progression toward reference-making speech. Lewis, on the other hand, has suggested that the use of the *mama* to express volition relates to the use of the name *mama* in distress cries. Another possibility is that *mama* represents a generalized agent in this context. The identity of *mama* to the word for "mother" does not seem critical, since Piaget cites an example of a child using his grandfather's name in demands. We have a number of examples in which a child uses *mama* to direct requests to people other than his mother.

In our treatment, we have distinguished the name *mama* from the Volitional marker *mama* on the basis of gestures and intonation. In an utterance with demand intonation, if the child reaches toward or otherwise gestures for his mother, *mama* is considered a Volitional Object, not a simple marker of Volition. On the other hand, if the child did not orient toward his mother but toward a desired object or location, *mama* is taken as a Volitional marker. In some later cases of *mama,* as a Volitional Object the child used *mama* with the intonation of adult Vocatives. More careful analysis of gestures and intonation, along with experimental work on the child's awareness of the role of agents in satisfying his demands, might allow a better definition of the uses of this word.

Nicky

Nicky's use of *mama* to express Volition, beginning at 13(19), does not refer to his mother, since, by then, he no longer called his mother *mama,* but rather called her by name. He used *mama* even for requests to his father, although he already had the word *dada* in his vocabulary.

During his first formal observation session, at 18(4), Nicky produces a number of two-word sequences, the first member of which is *mommy,* to express the attitude of desire, and the second member of which is the name of an indicated or desired Object. Each element of the sequence had already developed in one word speech: *mama* from 13(19) and Object words in Volitional contexts from 14 (12-18).

All the Volitional *mommy* sequences from Nicky I are presented in Table 15. The function of *mommy* in the first example is somewhat ambiguous, but the next example is clearly Volitional: Nicky repeatedly calls because he wants the *showel.* Whether *memmy* refers specifically to mother as a Vocative or Object of Volition in these examples, or still functions as a generalized request is unclear from our data. In support of the Volitional interpretation, however, is the report from his diary that, as recently as the week before the first formal observation session, Nicky had been using *mommy* to his father in situations where he wanted something. In the period between 16(25) and 17(1), Nicky said *daddy; mommy; daddy* when he wanted his father to pick him up. In this sequence, daddy appears to be the term of address, *mommy* the Volitional element. *Mama* as a volitional pivot ultimately drops out. Therefore, it seems best to think of *mama* and its variants as initially retaining an expressive quality characteristic of prelinguistic verbal communication, a kind of Performative with an unverbalized object. *Mama* is, thus the first instance of the Volitional Mode.

Matthew

Beginning around 12(8), Matthew began to use *mama* to request specific objects or actions. This usage is already productive during the initial formal observation period at 12(15,22), when there are eight unambiguous instances. These examples are presented in Table 9. The fact that Matthew is whining every time he says *mama* makes clear the volitional intent.

Table 8. Volitional sequences involving Mommy at Nicky 1-18(4)

Preceding context	Mod*ality*	Event
Fan is off.		
What's that? Fan	N banging *mommy*	fan ban
	N repeats *mommy*	
What do you want?		showel (shovel)
	M whining *mommy*	
What?	M reach*ing for* whining, repeats	*piggy* bank to put in penny *bappy* (bank)
	M reaching toward whining, repeats *mommy*	drawers on dresser *door*
What do you want?	M reaching for	*clock* *clock*

Mommy is a component of Matthew's first sequence of two single words on a related topic. At 15(11), Matthew calls *mommy*; his mother answers *What?* and he replies *down,* which is interpreted as an Action request. Note that in this conversational sequence, *mommy* functions conversationally as an adult Vocative.

Around 16(4-18), *mommy* is extensively used as an initial-position Volitional marker in early two-word sentences. *Mommy* was combined with names of objects such as *ball* and *cookie,* and actions such as *down.* Between 16(7) and 16(13), Matthew forms the sequence *mommy; daddy; mommy* in order to express a desire for his father, who is absent. Here, *mommy* is used in a situation similar to the earlier single-word instances, but is now combined sequentially with *daddy* as the Object of Volition. About two months later, at Matthew V-17(13), *mommy* becomes the first word to be used productively in the formation of sequences. During this observation session, *mommy* enters into five sequences with a variety of other words. In several of these, *mommy* is used in situations parallel to earlier uses of *mommy* as a general request term. For example, Matthew's mother asks *Do you want some spaghettios?* to which Matthew replies *Spaghettios,* followed by multiple repetitions of *mommy* in a whining intonation. As in Nicky's case, each of the component semantic functions was well established in one-word form before occurring together in a sequence.

Table 9. Uses of Mama at Matthew 1-12(15) and 12(22)

Preceding context	Modality		Event
	M pointing to whining *ma*		microphone
	M reaching for whining, repeats *mama*		orange juice glass
	M Looking at whining *mama*		bottle of milk
Mother holding doll	walks to whining *mama*		doll

	N reaching toward whining repeats *mama*	tape recorder
with mother in room, sitting on rocking chair that he has stopped rocking	M whining, repeats	(to be taken of)

No and Yeah

No was first used to accompany the performance of desired, but forbidden, actions. However, its most common use in a volitional context was to reject objects or events. Leopold has pointed out that children often show some initial confusion between *no* and *yes,* and use *no* to give an affirmative answer to questions. *yes* is only acquired much later in the course of linguistic developments.

Nicky

At 11(28), Nicky says *na; na* while crawling to a forbidden bookcase. At this early point in development, the expression of desire cannot be separated from the act of crawling toward the bookcase. Later, at 15(19), he says *no* when merely tempted to touch a forbidden object. Thus, the expression of desire has been separated from the action. However, it is still difficult to tell whether Nicky is expressing a negative prohibition or a positive desire to carry out the forbidden act.

At the time of Nicky's first observation session at 18(4), *no* is a productive word. All examples of his use of *no* in single-word, volitional utterances are presented in Table 10. The three instances of *no* that occur during the first session are all related to preceding verbal context. Thus, Nicky already has passed beyond the stage, recorded in his diary, at which *no* is only used in relation to situational context. Note that Nicky uses *no* to mean *yes* in response to the question *Do you want to go out in the backyard?* The affirmative nature of the reply is indicated by the fact that Nicky did not oppose going out and was, in fact, happy outside. Thus, although he earlier used *no* appropriately to signal rejection in relation to nonverbal context, when Nicky begins to respond to verbal queries, he uses *no* to signal both terms of the assent—refusal opposition. This confusion must be cleared up later, but our data do not throw light on the progression.

The next qualitative development in the volitional *no* is reported in Nicky's diary between 18(15) and 18(21). At this stage, Nicky uses *no* to express his will concerning the actions of others, not just himself; for instance, he says *no!* to tell other children not to touch his toy. Here, we have yet another example of a decentration process within the period of one-word speech. This usage of *no* is confirmed during the next formal observation sessions, Nicky II—18(27) and Nicky III—19(29), as the next example in Table 10 show.

According to diary observations, Nicky first used *no* in a two-word combination between 19(15) and 20(5). These combinations had single-sentence intonation and timing from their inception. The first such sentences used during a formal observation session occurred at Nicky III—19(29); they are given in Table 18. Note that, in the first example and in the complex sequence, Nicky is rejecting an Object. A number of earlier investigations also observed two-word utterances in which the object of the negative wish, previously unexpressed in single-word utterances, is added to the negative element. It is interesting that this sentences has no precedent in sequences. That is, no sequences occurred through Nicky III in which Nicky used *no* in a volitional context, followed by a word expressing a rejected Object or State. However, there is an interesting sequence at Nicky III in which a volitional *no* is followed by naming an object he is being denied. Nicky's mother, saying *Let's go down; let's get down,* takes him down from a chair from which he could watch the tape recorder. Nicky's response is *no!* followed by *cacor* to express the Object of a positive Volition.

The second and third examples in Table 5 superficially appear to involve rejection of an object. However, examination of the situational context reveals that Nicky probably is rejecting an action in which the object is involved. Thus, it appears that *no bappa,* far from indicating that Nicky doesn't want his diaper, indicates that he doesn't want his mother to do something to it. In the last four examples, he is rejecting an action in which he would be involved.

At Nicky IV—20(23), *no* is also productive in two-word utterances, occurring nine times in Volitional contexts, but there are a couple of new developments. One is that Nicky has been talking about his *hi cord* and then rejects it with the words *no hi.* Here, he uses *no* in connection with a word used to describe an attribute or State of the thing he is rejecting. This seems like an added level of cognitive embedding. Another new event is that the word *don('t)* appears, a more adult form of *no* in the Volitional context, as when his mother says *I'm really going to put on the hi record. It's really going to be that one;* and Nicky answers *don('t).* During this session, he also expresses the Volitional relation itself, saying *no wan(t),* again with reference to the "hi" record.

Finally, the first example of a three-word Volitional utterance involving *no* occurs: Nicky's mother has put on the "hi" record, and he responds *no; no hi.* His mother answers *Yes hi. You asked for hi;* and Nicky says *no want it.* Thus, we see an orderly progression in the expression of negative volition, from one to two- to three-word form; each step involves the addition of an element previously implicit in the situation.

An interesting example involving *no* appears in a complex sequence during Session IV. In this example, Nicky whines *no record* and follows with *off*. Here *off* serves a as kind of paraphrase of his previous statement.

The next period, Nicky V—21(17), manifests one new development in the volitional use of *no:* Nicky's mother is putting bread in her mouth, and Nicky responds by whining *mouth; bread; no mouth.* Here, for the first time, Nicky rejects a Location rather than an Object or Action.

At Nicky VI—22(21), we find a new variant of a three-word volitional message: *no more (ba) nana,* as Nicky hands his mother a banana. Here, *more* is an attribute of banana and the phrase *more banana* is subordinate to the Modal element, *no*.

At Nicky VII—23(21) there are several new types of Volitional utterances involving *no.* One of these is *no* in combination with a vocative. For example, Nicky's mother says *Now leave the candle there,* to which Nicky responds *no mama!* Another is *no* in a three-word utterance in which the Action is encoded in two words:

Mother	Nicky
Are you ready to run around?	*no run around*

At Nicky VIII-24(23), new variants of Volitional utterances with *no* appear. Nicky rejects an animate Object or Dative in the following complex sequence: Matthew is trying to get up on a stool, and Nicky responds, *no feet; no feet please; no feet Math.* He also uses *no* in several three-word utterances involving Agent's Action plus Object, as in *no push truck* when Matthew is about to push a truck. At the same time, *not* appears for the first time with a Volitional function; Nicky says *not on door* as Matthew is putting shapes on the door. Finally, *yeah* in a Volitional context makes its first appearance:

Mother	Nicky
You want to fo downstairs now?	*yeah; bye bye*

The development of the Volitional *no* in Matthew's speech is similar to its development in Nicky's. We shall discuss only those few aspects in which Matthew differed from Nicky or provided complementary information.

At Period III-15(5,17), Matthew uses the Volitional *no* in three out of four cases to reject situational events rather than verbal propositions. During this same session, Matthew also encodes an Object of negative, rather than positive Volition when he says *(s)poon,* pushing away a spoon. Here he encodes the Object of rejection rather than the attitude of rejection itself. In Chapter 4, we shall show that informational and presuppositional structure explain why rejection is more frequently encoded than the rejected objected object. In later sessions, nonexistence similarly was signaled both by the word *no* and by naming the nonexistence referent.

Negative Volition is much less frequent for Matthew than for Nicky. Matthew's infrequent use of *no* is compensated by his frequent use of the affirmative word *yeah,* a word almost never used by Nicky. *Yeah* first appears in a conversational sequence at Matthew V—17(13); Matthew whines *fishy,* pointing in their direction; his mother responds *Do you want to see the fish?* and he answers *yeah,* thus expressing positive Volition or desire. Affirmation is from the beginning an operation on a linguistic, not a situational structure. From Matthew VI—18(18), *yeah* is frequently used simply to answer questions about his desires, both in sequences and independently. An example of this occurs when Matthew replies *yeah* to his mother's question *Do you want to sit down at your table?*

Yeah continues to be used in later sequences, where it affirms desired actions as well as objects. For instance, at Matthew VI, he says *pour,* whining and pointing to a milk container. His mother responds *Do you want to pour?* and Matthew answers *yeah.* Whereas Matthew is affirming his own desired action here, he later uses *yeah* to affirm a desired act on the part of another person. At Matthew VII-19(21), the following sequence occurs: Matthew gives a spoon to his mother and says *cut.* She answers *Do you want me to cut?* and Matthew replies *yeah.* Thus, there is a proses of decentration in Matthew's Volitional use of *yeah,* just as there is for both boys' Volitional use of *no.* Affirmative Volition is also used in sequence in relation to semantic functions other than Objects and Actions. For instance, at Matthew VIII-20(26), Matthew whines *mommy,* trying to put in a puzzle piece; she answers *Do you want me to help?* and Matthew answers *yeah.* Thus, he expresses a desire for his mother to act as Agent. In this way, connected discourse expands along with other developmental changes.

Expression of the Volitional modality occurs only after the indicative has been established. The earliest examples of Volition involve using *no* to accompany forbidden actions. In later uses, Volition becomes an expression of mode separated from action and takes on an autonomous role.

Mama is used early by both boys as a general Volitional pivot to demand a wide variety of objects and actions. Although *mama* comes to be used in sequences, it commonly is used only to initiate a sequence, not to respond to a mother's inquiry. In later speech, *mama* does not become incorporated into two-word sentences, but rather moves toward a more clearly Vocative role.

The initial appearance of *no* in an adult usage is for the rejection of objects or actions in nonverbal contexts. Rejection is expressed first with regard to actions that directly concern the child; later, the child expresses volition regarding the action of others. Subsequently, *no* comes to be used in response to verbal context, namely, to answer yes—no questions. However, a positive yes—no question presupposes that both responses are equally probable, so neither alternative is marked. Thus, *no* is used to encode either assent or refusal. This early experience of relating *no* to words, not just to things, through structural combination of question and answer may explain why *no* is common in children's two-word speech.

Yeah appears later than *no* and serves to encode assent to yes-no questions. Matthew acquired *yeah* sooner and used it more frequently than Nicky. As in adult speech, *yeah* is not used in response to nonverbal contexts, since some alternative must be suggested verbally before *yeah* is appropriate.

The fact that exactly the same situational context is the basis for assigning a given semantic structure and content to utterances, whether they be expressed in one-word, two-word or three-word form. is evidence for a common underlying semantic structure at each level of syntactic complexity. For example, during Nicky's first observation session, in which he made no two-word utterances, he answers the question *would you like some fruit now?* with the single word *no*. During Nicky IV, he answers the question *Do you want a cracker?* with the two-word utterance *no cracker*. IN each case, a similar preceding verbalized question is taken as the source of the proposition which Nicky is opposing. There seems to be no reason to accept the preceding question as evidence of semantic structure in the second case, but to reject it in the first. *No cracker* is o less ambiguous than *no* alone, since, as Bloom points out, an utterance like *no cracker* is, without context, ambiguous among the three alternative readings: negative Volition, nonexistence, and denial. Structured situational context is equally necessary to a semantic interpretation in both single word and multiword situations.

Jakobson has suggested that the progression from *no* to *yes* is an example of development from an unmarked to a marked form: *Yes* represents a new level of specificity or marking because affirmation has been assumed before the emergence of the affirmative word. The negative by contrast is not assumed, so negative marking must be used to signal the contrary of an event or proposition.

This formulation and our findings show a fascinating congruence with a theoretical formulation of adult processing of negatives by Wason. Synthesizing a heretofore heterogeneous and confusing set of results from many experiments, Wason concludes that the natural function of a negative proposition is to signal a change in meaning, whereas the natural function of an affirmative proposition is to signal constancy of meaning. Before this, negative processing had been conceptualized in terms of grammatical and logical transformations necessary to bridge the gap between sentence and state of affairs. But this approach did not really work, as Wason shows. His conclusion fits perfectly with our results on the origins of negative and affirmative form and function in children. In its Volitional function, as well as other semantic functions described in other sections, *no* is used "to contradict or correct; to cancel a suggestion of one's own or another's," as Strawson, in Wason, the philosopher, said. Wason states that negatives function in an affirmative context. The same holds true even when the context is nonverbal—both Nicky and Matthew begin by rejecting unwanted actions. Just like adults, they are not describing the present state of affairs, but negating it. Precisely the same holds true when negatives begin to relate to verbal context in a dialogue situation: *No* is used to contradict or correct someone else' verbal suggestion. Wason has shown how, even at adulthood, when the negative is part of one's own sentence, this is still the primary or natural function of the negative. Similarly, our data on the origins of *yes* show that affirmative marking arises to signal constant meaning.

When children begin to answer yes—no questions relating to Volition, their first response is the unmarked affirmative: Analysis of data from Matthew shows that he repeats the key word in the proposition. The earliest examples are at Matthew II—14(10,18) as in this exchange:

Mother	Matthew
Do you want to get up?	*up*

This first stage is the most unmarked form, the simple affirmative proposition. Furthermore, it signals *constancy* of meaning in the most direct way possible—by repeating the key word in the proposition. The next stage is the marked negative, no. Here is an example from Matthew III—15(5,17):

Mother	Matthew
(carrying Matthew upstairs)	(whinning)
Can you walk upstairs	*no; no*

No is marked relative to the simple affirmative proposition, repeated by the child at the earlier stage. It also differs from the earlier affirmative in signaling change or opposition to the proposition contained in the question. The final stage is the marked affirmative *yeah,* first appearing at Matthew VI—18(18), for instance:

Mother	Matthew
Do you want to pour	*yeah*

Again, the affirmative signals constancy of meaning, even in its new marked form. Thus, there is a clear three-step progression toward the acquisition of increasingly marked forms, exactly in accord with Jakobson's concept of marking. At the same time, the earliest form of affirmation—repetition—dramatically concretize Wason's idea that the affirmative signals constancy of meaning, while the Volitional use of *no* indicates that negatives do, in fact, signal a change in meaning relative to a positive context.

Both Wason's and Jakobson's formulations are confirmed by the development of the child's responses to yes—no questions of a Volitional nature. The continuity between the origins of the negative and affirmative operations and their later use appears to be of great theoretical significance. It indicates that the structural origins of language in one-word speech are basic to mature adult linguistic competence and might even offer clues as to its nature.

Volitional objects

Children ask for specific people or objects only after the naming function is firmly established. Guillaume pointed out the existence of such single-word utterances expressing the object of a demand. Although we have chosen to separate Performative Objects according to mode-Indicative or Volitional—clearly, the distinction between animate and inanimate Objects also is important, for the vocative may be defined as an animate Volitional Object. We have refrained from organizing our material in terms of both distinctions for simplicity of presentation rather than for theoretical reasons.

Nicky

Nicky's first use of a Volitional Object is unique in involving interrogative intonation. Between 14(12) and 14(18), while his mother is hospitalized, he goes around the house saying *Do(t)?* while looking for her. A second example occurs between 15(19) and 16(18), when he says *Ke(lly),* trying to call a friend named Kelly.

Between 16(19) and 16(25), Nicky's diary first notes a demand in which an inanimate Object of Volition is given verbal expression—Nicky uses *maw* or *naw* to demand milk. Thus, expression of the Object of Volition emerges after expression of the Volitional attitude by *mama*. The delay is not due to lack of vocabulary, since a child often can label an object before he asks for it.

During Nicky's first observation session, there are a number of examples of the Vocative type of Volitional Object. For example, at one point he indicates a picture and says *mommy;* seems to express a demand for attention. When the mother's attention is secured. Nicky follows with an Indication.

Instances of volitional objects at Nicky VII-23 (21)

Preceding context		*Modalit*	*Event*
	N	going to get	diaper *diaper*
	N	whining	*cracker, cracker*
	N	reaching for	*eggs* *eggs*
	N	reaching for repeats	lid *lid*
What are you looking for?	N	points to	Picture of Doogle *Doogle*
	N	going over to whining	bike *bike*
Where are you going to?			*library*
	N	looking for whining, repeats	letters *C*
	N	looking for whining	something *C*

By the time of Nicky's first observation session at 18(4), he is already using inanimate Volitional Objects in response to verbal context. However, he continues to express objects of volition in combination with nonverbal elements throughout the period under study. During this first session, whining, reaching, and repetition all are used to indicate the Volitional mode. For example, on one occassion, Nicky says *mil(k)* while reaching for milk. On another, he answers the question *Any more milk?* by whining and saying *(ba)nana.* On a third, he answers the same question by repeating *(ba)nana, (ba)nana.* A child often will repeat a demand until he gets what he wants; the fact that the child stops his repetition validates the mother's interpretation of the child's utterance. Some idea of the variety and productivity of this function is given in Table 19, which presents all the reliable instances at Nicky VII-23(21)—the formal session at which this semantic function is used most frequently. Note that locomotion toward an object, as well as reaching for it, is considered an expression of the Volitional attitude. Functionally, the two appear identical; the only difference is that reaching involves only the hand, whereas locomotion toward an object involves the whole body.

The first use of a Volitional Object in a sequence occurs after isolated Volitional Objects are well established. Our first example is the *mommy; showel* sequence at 1—18(4) described in Section 3.5. In the course of the following session, Nicky II—18(27), Nicky used his first two-word sentences combining the expression of Volition with Object of Volition. One good example is *awa(nt) pretzel,* as he reaches for a pretzel. The situation is of exactly the same type as those in which single-word Volitional utterances have occurred previously.

Matthew

In his earliest use of *mama*, Matthew seemed to use

mama as a vocative simply to ask his mother to come. This phenomenon was reported in his diary, at 9(16), when he greeted his mother with *mamama* while gesturing that he wanted her. Matthew's diary first mentions him reaching for an inanimate object which he names—*c(r)acke(r)*—at 12(23). Objects of Volition are produced my Matthew in every formal session except the second. For Matthew, as for Nicky, the performative elements of reaching, whining, and repeating are used in combination with Object names. At 13(23), it was noted in Matthew's diary that he was starting to point at, rather than reach toward, Objects of Volition. At this point, it seems as though Matthew is able to rely on relatively more verbal cues—intonation and repetition—to express Volition. Table 20 presents all the reliable examples of Volitional Objects from Matthew V—17(13), the session in which he produced the largest number. These examples illustrate the productivity of this semantic function.

Matthew first uses a Volitional Object in a sequence between 16(7) and 16(13); the *mommy; daddy; mommy* example from the diary described in Section 3.5. At 17(11), he is reported to answer a question by expressing a Volitional Object of Performative Action. His mother asks *Where are you going?* and Matthew answers *(f)ishy* as he goes downstairs to the aquarium at the foot of the stairs. Remember that "moving towards" is considered a performative expression of Volition and note that this element is present in both his mother's question and Matthew's action.

At Matthew VIII—20(26), we find the first multiword utterance in which both Volition and its Object are expressed verbally. Reaching toward his mother's coffee, Matthew says *I wa(nt) some.* Note that the reaching gesture is present in the volitional situation just as it was in many earlier single-word utterances in which Object of Volition was the only element linguistically encoded.

Instances of volitional objects at Matthew V-17(13)

Preceding context		*Modality*	*Event*
	M	whining, repeats	*fishy*
	M	whining, repeats	*fishy*
	M	looking around for whining	*bottle* *bottle*
	M	whining	*bottle*
Bananas are on table	M	pointing to whining	bananas *(ba)nana*
	M	reaching for whining	banana *bananas*
	M	reaching up towards	mother *mommy*
	M	whining, repeats	*(spaghett)io(s)*
Sitting on mother	M	whining, repeats	*cookie*
	M	looking at mother whining, repeats	*cookie*
	M	running & pointing to whining	record player *cacord,cacord*(record)
Record player is off.	M	running to	record player *record*
	M	whining	*milk*
	M	pointing to whining	door *door*
	M	whining, repeats	*door*

Door is open.	M	whining	*door*
	M	reaching for whining	refrigerator door *door*
	M	reaching towards	drawer *drawer*

Volitional Objects have the same event structure as Indicative Objects, but involve different modality elements. Both boys produce their first Volitional Objects after Indicative Objects are established in their speech, and express animate Volitional Objects before inanimate ones.

Object of Volition is a very productive semantic relation for both boys, involving a wide variety of combinations of verbal and situational elements. The single-word Object of Volition is expressed first in isolation and is used later as a response in dialogue. It also comes to represent but one aspect of the situation encoded sequentially by several single-word utterances. Finally, Volition and its Object both are expressed together in two-word utterances, in situations having a nonverbal structure exactly like that which characterized earlier utterances. Once again we find a systematic progression from single words to syntax. During this progression, the child comes to use words in response to verbal context and to encode more than one aspect of a given event.

Agent

Agents are expressed infrequently by either boy as isolated single-word utterances, as Table 3 and 4 show. Our explanation for this is that children usually do not express situational elements that can be taken for granted. Thus, an Agent will be expressed only where its identity cannot be assumed, that is, under conditions of uncertainty, in the information theory sense, where *from the point of view of the child* there are alternative Agents possible in the situation. Since the identity of an Agent usually can be taken for granted, Agents are expressed infrequently. This is especially likely in the case of the child's own actions.

Nicky

In the earliest examples, a sound made by an absent person is identified by naming that person. In this situation, the Agent is not present, so his identity is maximally uncertain. For Nicky, an instance of this type is recorded in his diary at 13(3), when he goes to the door upon hearing someone coming in, and says *dada*. Because his father already is present in the room, this instance is somewhat ambiguous, but we do know from another study that, at this time, Nicky referred to people other than his father as *dada*. A more clear-cut instance is reported in the diary around the time of the first formal observation. Between 18(1) and 18(8), Nicky says *auwen* upon hearing her voice outside. The name is an Agent in the sense that it answers the question *Who is making the noise?* A similar example occurs during the formal session itself. At 18(4), when asked the question *Did you hear them outside?*, Nicky answers *Ma(tthew)* upon hearing crying outside. Once again, the earliest nonimitative examples of a semantic function are stimulated by situational context alone; only later does verbal context become part of the stimulating situation. As in this case, verbal context often combines with, rather than replaces, the nonverbal structure of the situation.

The next example, from Nicky's diary between 18(19) and 18(25), involves an Agent who is present, but uncertain for other reasons. Nicky's mother had been playing "Ring around the Rosy" with Nicky and Matthew. Nicky wanted to play again, so his mother took his hands, ready to play. Nicky broke away and said *Ma(tthew),* then was content when all three played together. In this example, Matthew had been excluded as active participant or Agent in the game, and Nicky was signaling a desired *change* of Agent. Thus, the function Agent is used here in a volitional context.

During the formal session that follows—II 18(27), Agents are expressed sequentially for the first time in the following conversation. The situation is like earlier ones in that absent Agents are involved.

Mother	Nicky
(Doorbell rings	
There's someone coming in	*wawa* (Lauren)
Mmm. That's Lauren out there	*mama* (Matthew)
And Matthew too.	*ma(tthew)*
And Matthew too.	

Thus, we find once more an orderly progression from single-word utterance to sequence.

Note that in all the examples thus far, Nicky has not named himself as Agent. This is further confirmation that a role that is assumed or presupposed will be less likely to be linguistically encoded at an earlier stage. We would expect the decentration process, described in earlier sections, to lead to the expression of self as Agent at a later point in development. For Nicky, encoding his own body parts is apparently an intermediate stage in becoming aware of, and encoding himself as, Agent. At Nicky III—19(29), Nicky says *hand,* referring to his hand holding crayons. *Hand* is considered an Agent because it is the animate instigator of the holding action.

During this same session, a conversational sequence occurs in which, for the first time, Agent and Action are sequentially encoded in a series of single word utterances. Nicky says *owl,* looking at a picture of an owl to which his mother is pointing. Mother echoes *That's an owl,* to which Nicky responds *tootoo,* thus expressing the owl's Action. In this sequence, *owl* has a dual function. In relation to the situation, *owl* functions as Object of Indicative Action, but once Nicky has said *tootoo, owl* can be thought of as the Agent. The correspondence between word and thing embodied in Indicative Objects is intrinsic to the expression of more complex semantic functions. As has been the case for other sequences described up to now, each semantic function had been established earlier in isolated single-word form before appearing as a member of a sequence.

Not until Nicky VI—22(21) does Nicky name himself as Agent. On three occasions, he says *Nicky*— once going to get up on a chair; once trying to climb on the bed; and once chasing Matthew. At this point, the decentration of the Agent function is complete.

During this same session, we find the first Agent—Action two-word utterances: Nicky, waiting for Matthew to push a toy to him, says *Nicky catch;* Nicky, lying in bed, says to his mother, who is not in bed, *memmy sleep.* Thus, the progression from single-word utterance to sequence to sentence is completed for the Agent function.

Matthew

At 13(3), Matthew is reported to say *dady* upon hearing his father come in the outside door and start up the steps to his apartment. Thus, Matthew, like Nicky, starts by expressing the absent Agent. This type of example is described several more times in the diary in the next month or so. Matthew's use of the Agent is so infrequent in the observation sessions that we must rely on the diary to chart the development of Matthew's expression of Agent.

At 16(17), Matthew expresses Agent in a sequence when, addressing his mother, he says *mommy; daddy* as his father starts to sharpen a knife. In another example, at 19(14), Matthew has been trying unsuccessfully to cut his meat with a knife when he hands the knife, an instrument, to his mother, saying *mommy.* Here, the Agent case is again used to signal a desired *change* of actor. Another example illustrates the same point, but both alternative Agents are verbalized. At 20(10), Matthew's sister Lauren says *Let me do it;* Matthew answers *mommy,* explicitly replacing the Agent of the verbal context, *me,* with *mommy.* This type of contrast of one Agent with another, alternative Agent is frequent. Clearly, the children verbalize an Agent when it will be informative, in the information theory sense of partitioning alternatives. At 17(2), Matthew forms his first sequence involving an Agent and an Action: *(f)ishy; ea(t)* while watching the fish eat. Both component functions had appeared earlier in isolated single word form. At 17(12), Matthew is reported to have formed his first Agent—Action two-word utterance: He says *daddy bye-bye* after his father has left for work. Here we have the completion of the now familiar progression from single-word, to sequence, to multiword utterance.

The expression of an Agent in response to a verbal

question is first reported at 18(3), long after the first instances involving situational context, but also after the onset of multiword utterances; this latter fact constitutes a small inconsistency in the data. The instance is part of a conversational sequence: Matthew says *gong* in the middle of dinner. His mother answers *Are the people gone?* Matthew replies *birdy.* In fact, the pet canary had died and been buried that day.

It can be seen that all are situations in which the Agent cannot be taken for granted: The Agent either is absent or his identity is in question. It is, perhaps, because this situational requirement rarely is met that Agent is expressed in isolated single-word form with relative rarity. When a relatively long-absent person is named, it often is hard to tell what semantic role the child has in mind. Because such instances usually had to be eliminated for lack of context, the number of Agents may have been disproportionately reduced. This fact does not detract in any way from our analysis of the relatively clear-cut instances.

Matthew's first verbal expression of self as Agent is the final step in the Agent development, as it was for Nicky, Unlike Nicky, however, Matthew, at 19(3), takes this step in the context of a two-word utterance: He says *me (l)igh(t)* in a situation where he wants to turn the light on.

The expression of Agent in single-word form is relatively infrequent for Matthew and Nicky. Especially at the early stages, it mainly seems limited to situations where the Agent cannot be taken for grant by the children. This state of affairs excludes the encoding of self as Agent; however, with development, there is a decentration process such that both boys eventually name themselves as Agents.

The first examples for both boys involved identification of an absent person who can be heard. These examples are Indicative; later Volitional examples involve expression of a desire for a change of Agent. These findings were confirmed by Veneziano in a study of two children acquiring Italian. She found that verbalization of the Agent was relatively infrequent, and that it often was expressed in situations where change of Agency was involved or where there was evidence that the child was aware of alternative Agents.

The earliest nonimitative expression of Agents is a response to situational context; later, Agents also may be expressed in response to verbal context. There is, too, a regular progression from isolated one-word utterance to sequence to sentence in the verbal expression of the Agent function.

Action or state of an agent

Children typically describe their own actions before they describe those of other Agents. As an ideal type, Action or State of an Agent differs from the earliest Performatives, on the border of language proper, in that there is a more clear-cut and language-like separation of word and act: the Action word *refers* to the act rather than being *part* of it. This separation, however, appears gradually, as Nicky's earliest example shows.

The first words used to encode Action or State often are not verbs. Leopold observed that adult adverbs were used before verbs in both English and German. It was findings like these that led him to despair of using parts of speech as a framework for analyzing early language.

Guillaume also observed that, in French, both verbs and other forms in adult syntax were used by children to encode the same action.

Nicky

Nicky first labels an Action at 13(30), when he says *do(wn)*, sitting down in the appropriate place in the "Ring around the Rosy" game. At this point, *down* still has characteristics of a "pure' Performative because it is part of a social routine. Between 14(21) and 15(18), he is reported to use this word *down* while going down steps or sitting down. This is the first proper instance of Action or State of an Agent. Between 16(25) and 17(1), Nicky begins to say *u(p)* while going up a step. Between 17(1) and 17(17), he uses the word *dag* to describe his action as he walks backwards. At the time of the first formal observation, 18(4), Nicky says up while reaching up to the fan. The performative element of reaching indicates that the word *up*, which describes Nicky's intended action, is embedded in a volitional context. The Action or State word *up* is thus part of a more complicated cognitive structure involving both demand and description of action. During the same session, Nicky says *hot* while starting to eat hot soup. This type of usage has been classed as Action or State of Agent rather than Object because the child changes state to hot. If this were a description of the Object, it would represent a constant-state description, a development that occurs much later. At Period II—18(27), Action or State of an Agent is expressed spontaneously 18 times. *Down* is the principle vocabulary item, being used in a range of situations. Table 22 presents all the different usages of *down* at this time. One notable feature of the table is that it records Nicky using *down* when he is getting up, on six occasions. Because the child—speaker is always the Agent in these early expressions of instigated action, the degree of separation between word and act is hard to assess. Encoding his own Action or State can thus be seen as a transitional mechanism that helps the child separate word from act and ultimately leads to the generalized verbal encoding of Actions and States.

During this session, for the first time, Nicky encodes Action of Agent in a nonimitative response to verbal context. His mother asks *Where are you going?* and Nicky answers *down* as he gets down from a chair. Once again, the ability to express a given semantic function in relation to a verbal element follows the ability to express it in relation to a situation one.

A new semantic development is reported in Nicky's diary between 18(25) and 19(1): Nicky uses *down* when he wants someone else to pick him up or put him down. Here, *down* describes the Action or State of a Dative rather than an Agent. Because these instances are rare, they have not been placed in a separate category.

During the next formal session, III-19(29), Nicky first encodes the Action or State of an Agent other than himself. This happens in response to a question from his mother: *Do you want to hear the dog go woof woof?* Nicky responds *quack quack*. This utterance involves paradigmatic substitution—*quack quack* for *woof woof*—rather than the syntagmatic completion of the earlier dialogue. It is also the first example of encoding Action or State in a situation which involves a process rather than change of state. There are several other examples in this same session. One involves a more standard sort of verb: Nicky says *bay* a number of times during an extended complex sequence in connection with playing in the water.

Between 20(3) and 20(10), a new type of usage appears. Semantically, it could perhaps best be categorized as what Filmore terms the Factitive, the object or being resulting from an Action or State. Nicky says *dot* while drawing some dots; he also says *cr(oss)* when he wants his mother to draw a cross for him. These observations are confirmed by the next formal session, Nicky IV—20(23), when the following two examples occur:

1. Nicky, about to draw a cross, says *cro(ss).*
2. *Nicky's mother asks* What are you going to draw? and Nicky answers *dot,* proceeding to draw some.

These examples are treated as a special type of Action or State of Agent because of their rarity. Although a case could be made for treating them as a special type of Object of Action, it probably is most revealing to think of them as a new type, combining features from both types of semantic function. Because *cro(ss)* and *dot* describe the child's movement as well as its result, these Factitives were placed with Action or State of Agent rather than with Objects of Action. It is interesting that the result of an action should first appear after the two more differentiated categories—Action or State of Agent and Object of Action—whose features it combines. This pattern is repeated by Instrument of Action, an amalgam of Agent and Object, described later in this chapter.

During session V—21(17), Nicky first expresses a transitive action where both Agent and Object are communicated in a message. The examples all involve the word *touch.* In one example, Nicky points to the tape recorder and says *touch.* Here that tape recorder is implied as Object by the gesture of pointing, while the word *touch* implies Nicky as an Agent. This attainment involves a development from a one-place predicate to a two-place predicate. Although one might posit an alternative interpretation of this usage as representing a development from *adverbial to verbal* encoding of action or State, such an interpretation is not supported by the facts, for Nicky had used the verb *dance* much earlier in an intransitive sense.

Nicky VI—22(21) represents the height of Nicky's productivity for Action or State of Agent. Table 23 presents all the examples of this function occuring in Nicky VI in isolated one-word form. The development of Nicky's ability to encode process where before he was limited to change of state is best illustrated by Nicky's use of *jump* when he is about to jump. A few months earlier, he would most likely have communicated his intention with *down.* Nicky points to a picture of a bear in bed and says *night night.* Since he has not seen the bear go to bed, it seems that he must be encoding the present constant state of the bear rather than process or change of state. Another similar, but more convincing, example occurs when Nicky says *rest* as he points to a picture of a bear resting.

Nicky VI also sees the appearance of the first two-word utterances encoding Agent plus Action. These have already been described in the preceding section on Agents. At the same time, there are also two-word utterances which encode the action and resultant State, each by a separate word. An example occurs when Nicky, about to get down, says *get down.*

Matthew

Matthew's development of Action or State of an Agent

parallels Nicky's. The first example occurs at 13(16) in an imitative context: Matthew's mother asks *Do you want to get up?* and he reaches up and says *up*. The gesture indicates that he understood the question. The first nonimitative instance to be recorded in Matthew's diary occurred at 14(5) when he said *night(t) night(t)* while getting ready for bed. Action or State of an Agent also appears in Matthew II-14(10, 18). Action of an Agent is a productive relation, but it occurs nonimitatively only in connection with the word *down*. ON three of these occasions, *down* is used in a situation in which an adult would use *up*.

During this same session, we find our first example of expression of Action or State of Agent in nonimitative response to verbal context. Matthew's mother asks *Do you want to get up?* and Matthew, about to climb up, answers *down*. These examples illustrate the verbal nondifferentiation of opposite poles of a dimension.

Again mirroring Nicky's developmental sequence, Matthew next embeds Action or State of Agent in the Volitional mode. This occurs a number of times at Matthew III-15(6,17). A representative example occurs when Matthew whines *dow(n)* while trying to get up on a chair. During the same session, Matthew encodes an Action or State of which he is the Dative rather than the Agent. In this example, Matthew, standing on a chair, reaches to him mother and says *down*. Here, Matthew indicates his mother as Agent, himself as Dative.

Encoding the Action or State of another person emerges next of Matthew, as it did for Nicky. At Matthew IV—16(2), he uses *bye bye* on two occasions when two different people are preparing to leave the house. It is not addressed to the people who are leaving, but is, rather a description of their Action or State change.

At this same time, Matthew, like Nicky, forms a sequence involving Action or State of an Agent, although the second word encodes Object or Location rather than Agent. In this example, a woman is going out the door and Matthew says *bye bye,* followed by *door*. The first example of the use of this function in a two-word sentence was at 16(5), when Matthew said *mommy down* when he wanted to get down from somewhere.

Transitive Action or State is the next development for Matthew. In the period from 16(16) to 16(30), Matthew begins to say *ea(t),* pointing to food, when he wants to eat. *Eat* is also the first word used to encode a process rather than a change of state. During this same period, at 16(21), Matthew encodes for the first time a constant state of an Agent: He says *dirty,* pointing to a spot on his arm.

At 17(2), Matthew is reported to form his first sequence involving both Agent and Action or State. Watching the fish eat, Matthew says *(f)ishy; ea(t).* Matthew's next development is to produce a two-word Agent—Action-or-State utterance. At 17(12), Matthew is reported to have said *Daddy bye bye* after his father left for work. Between 17(16) and 17(29), Matthew was recorded as saying *I see* when he wanted to see something. At this stage, there was no independent justification for segmenting this utterance. *See* is often reported in the literature and may serve as an Indicative marker. However, in this example, the Volitional context means that *I see* is a complex performative involving both Indicative and Volitional elements.

Shortly thereafter, at Matthew VI—18(18), a two-word utterance occurs in which Action and resultant State each are encoded by a distinct word. In answer to the question *Where'd the ice go?*, Matthew answers *go bye bye.*

At the same time, Matthew uses *eeah* to affirm an Action or State of an Agent for the first time. In one of a number of examples. Matthew's mother asks *Is Bernice writing?* and Matthew answers *yeah.* In interpreting *yeah* as affirming *writing*, we are assuming that Bernice's identity is presupposed by Matthew, and, therefore, is not the element being affirmed. This seems like a valid assumption, as Bernice Laufer, the observer, was well known to Matthew by this time.

Matthew;s first factitive occurred at Matthew VIII—20(26) as part of a conversational sequence. He is digging in the sand with a stick and says *house,* presumably referring to the result of his activity with the sand. Thus, Factitives occur, but with rarity for Matthew as well as for Nicky.

Action or State of Agent reaches its highest productivity in isolated one-word form during Matthew VIII-20(26).

The examples involving *no* and *yeah* deserve some explanation: *No* and *yeah* have here been used to deny or affirm an Action or State of an Agent, *no* for the very first time. Although Nicky had used *no* in denying an Object's identity, he never used *no* to deny an Agent's Action or State, nor did he ever affirm an Agent's Action or State with *yeah* or *yes*. An example of the expression of an Action and an Object occurs at Matthew IX—22(1)

Instances of action or state of agent at Matthew VIII-20(26)

Preceding context	Modality	Event
M is about to run over to sand.		*look*
	M	about to get down *down*
	M	getting down *down*
	M	getting down *down*
	M	getting down *down*
	M	getting down *down, down*
	M	picks up crib *sleep*
	M	reaching towards mother *up*
	M	climbing up on block *up*
	M	climbing up *up*

		M	climbing up on slide *up*
		M	climbs up on slide *up*
Where did Ismenia go?			*bye bye*
Where did baby go?			*bye bye*
		M	finishes drinking his milk *finished*
		M	about to walk on block *walk*
	M gives	mother	cookie *eat*
	M has gives	pigeons	bread *eat*
	M holding up whining repeating	banana	to cut *cut*
	M holds up	banana for mother	to cut
	M whining, repeats M touches		*cut* *hot* bench

when Matthew, about to look out the window, says *see it.*

Both Nicky and Matthew begin by describing their own Actions or States as they move, in an almost Performative manner. From here, their development proceeds in a number of directions. Both describe their own actions in a non verbal context before they do so in response to verbal context. Both boys also express a desired Action or State only after they have encoded their own current Action or State. From here, they go on to request Actions or changes of State from others, when they ask their mothers to pick them up or put them down; finally, they describe the Actions or States of other Agents. This sequence agrees with Guillaume's observation that children encode their own actions before those of others.

Almost none of the words first used to encode Action can be verbs in adult English, in which *up, down,* and *back* function as adverbs of direction and prepositions of location. When a child uses them in isolation, it is not clear whether they are referring to their direction of movement or the resultant location. *Down* said while jumping down could refer to the act of jumping or to its destination. It is thus difficult to decide on an objective basis whether *down* refers to an Action or a resultant State; we have formed a single semantic category to cover both at this stage of development. It is probably most accurate to say that Action and resultant State are not differentiated, that the child is basically attending to change, as P. Harris has suggested. Action and resultant State are more differentiated aspects of the basic category of perceived change. The fact that the child, jumping down, encodes the event with *down* rather than *jump* suggests that the child is focusing on the *change of State rather than the* Action itself, thus reinforcing our hypothesis. In other words, at the initial stages, the child is encoding the contrast between starting point and end point and is unable to encode either the intervening process or end point in isolation. This could explain why *down* is used to signal change in either direction. Vertical movement always implies a contrast between 'up' and 'down'.

Both boys pass through a stage in which *down* is used when getting up or down. This agrees with the observations of Leopold and Lewis that there is a stage of confusion between *up* and *down,* where one word is used to signal the vertical dimension. This is similar to the case of *no,* in that one pole of a dimension is used to represent the entire dimension before it is restricted to a specific pole. This phenomenon has been demonstrated experimentally with older children acquiring other pairs of polar opposites.

Whereas the earliest words referring to an Action of an Agent seem to encode a change of stage, later words encode intransitive process, transitive processes, and, last of all, constant states. Factitives such as *cross* may represent object nominalizations, another line of development of expression of Action or State. The final development for both boys was the concurrent expression of an action and a direction or resultant state in sentences such as *get down* and *go bye bye*.

Veneziano's data confirm this basic progression for children learning to speak Italian. She finds that pure action words like *tira* appear later in circumstances where words like *via* had been used earlier. Still later, both types are combined in two-word sentences.

As with other functions, both Nicky and Matthew start out by expressing single words, later use words in sequences, and finally combine them in two-word sentences.

Object

Object involved in direct action or state change is a developmental outgrowth of the Performative Object, and presupposes the basic referential relationship between word and thing involved in Indicative Objects. Objects differ from Performative Objects in that Performative Objects are not themselves affected by performative gestures such as pointing and reaching, whereas Objects are directly involved in an action which involves change of state. It is thus the character of the action or state associated with a given utterance that determines whether it was classified as a Performative Object.

Nicky

For Nicky, the first clear instance of naming and inanimate Object of a direct action is reported in his diary, between 16(19) and 16(25) when he says *bar*, demanding a fan be turned on or off. This first example corresponds to what Guillaume identified as an "object of intended action." The first examples of his naming an inanimate Volitional Object occur during the same period, so it is perhaps best to think of the two types of Object as undifferentiated at this point, especially since both occur in a Volitional context. There are two examples of Object in the first observation session. In one, Nicky says *dat,* playing with some blocks. In another, Nicky picks up his ball and says *ball.* This example shows that Performative and Direct Action form a continuum, for picking up could also function as Indicative Action.

Between 18(8) and 18(16), Nicky produces his first sequence involving an Object and its Action when he says *ban* followed by *ong*. His mother reports that he evidently expected the fan to be turned on after naming the Object. When nothing happened, he added the Action or State, and his mother complied. Both semantic functions making up the sequence had appeared earlier as isolated single-word utterances. In the next formal session, Nicky II—18(27), five sequences occur which include expression of an inanimate Object of action. One example is *cacoo* followed by *on*, said while going toward, and pointing to, a record player that was turned off. During this same session, we find the first instance of expressing Object in response to verbal context. Nicky's mother asks *Do you want it on?* and Nicky responds *acacor*.

Nicky's first two-word utterance, combining an inanimate Object with its Action or State, is reported in Nicky's diary between 20(10) when he begins to say *boo(k) back* to accompany the putting of books, records, and toys back on their shelf. Evidently, the word *book* had an extended referential meaning at this stage. In this same period, a new type of sequence involving an Object is reported. Nicky says *mi(tten)* as his mittens are being put on, followed by *co(ld)*. It appears that *co(ld)* is being used to express the function or cause of the mittens.

Objects are most numerous at Nicky VI—22(21). Table 25 presents the examples from this session in isolated one-word form, enabling the reader to realize the large range of combinatorial possibilities of word and event.

There is one particular Object that deserves special mention, the Locative Object; that is, an Object that seems to function as the Location of an Agent. The only one-word examples occur fairly late in the period under study, at Nicky VI—22(21). It is clear that the operational distinction between Locative and other Objects often seem to be just slightly larger Objects or to be both a Location and a manipulative Object. For this reason, and because the Locative Objects of this sort were rare for both boys, they have not been put in a separate category. A particular type of Locative, Location of Object, was defined in terms of a relation between two inanimate Objects. It was more frequent, as well as operationally distinct, and will be discussed as a separate category in a later section.

Matthew

In the case of Matthew, the first report of an inanimate Object directly involved in an action or state change occurs in his diary about a week after he first named an inanimate Object of Volition. At that time, 13(0), Matthew said *ba(ll),* having just thrown it. Matthew first expresses Object during a formal session at Matthew II—14(10, 18). In one of the two examples, Matthew turns on a record player and says *ca.* At 14(28), Matthew forms something like a sequence involving an Object and its Action. He says *car,* playing with toy cars and then *bye bye,* looking out the window. This sequence seems almost like a chain of association. Action or State of Object had already made its appearance in isolated form, so the sequence consisted of two preexisting semantic functions.

The next day, 14(29), Matthew forms two single-word utterances that seem to involve word combination *within* instead of *between* words. Matthew says *kye kye* playing with his toy cars and, at another time, *kye bye* while making the toy cars move. These utterances seem to represent some sort of amalgamation of *car* and *bye bye*.

The first example of a two-word utterance expressing Object plus its Action or State occurs at 15(27): *more meh* when he wants his bottle refilled.

Objects become most numerous at Matthew IV—16(2). Table 26 presents the examples from this session and illustrates the variety of combinations of named Objects with Actions or State Changes.

At Matthew VI—18(18), he first relates an Object to verbal context. Matthew's mother asks *What are you doing with that?* and Matthew answers *bu(tton),* pushing a button.

There are few examples of Objects in isolated single-word form which could be considered Locative Objects: At Matthew IV—16(2), Matthew says *door* when he is about to go out a *door*. At Matthew VIII—20(26), Matthew says *stone* walking on a stone.

Numerous examples of two-word utterances expressing Object plus State change occur at Matthew VIII—20(26); they are presented in Table 27. Note that, in each of these, the process word identifies an Action or State of the Object rather than the Agent. Thus, these examples are continuous with examples from one-word speech, but distinct from examples discussed in Section 3.8, Action or State of Agent, such as *eat cookie*. Another interesting point about the examples depicted in the Table is that each one conforms to adult word order whether this requires Object first or last. Thus, Matthew seems to be acquiring syntax, as his underlying semantic—conceptual structures come to be expressed more fully in linguistic form.

Instrumental objects

At 15(10), Matthew is reported to say *bu(tton)* after he pushes a turntable button and the record turntable has begun to revolve. *Here,* bu(tton) could be considered as Instrumental Object. In adult grammar, inanimate Objects may function as the Instrument of an Action, as well as its recipient. Fillmore identifies the Instrumental as "the case of the inanimate force or object causally involved in the action or state identified by the verb". In the case of one-word utterances, the action or state must be identified without the help of any verb, as we already have pointed out. Otherwise, however, the underlying concept guiding our search for the Instrumental case was the same as Fillmore's definition. In addition to the *bu(tton)* example, Matthew presented only one clear-cut case in isolated one-word form. At IV—16(2), Matthew said *(s)poon* while eating chips with a spoon. At 18(25), Matthew formed a two-word utterance involving a spoon as Instrument: Holding a spoon and pointing to the cabinet where his medicine was, he said *ea(t) (s)poon.* At Matthew VII—19(21), an Instrumental Object is produced as part of a complex sequence: Although these individual examples are interesting, the Instrumental did not really achieve productivity. Nicky produced no clear examples of instrument at all. Thus, it seems best to consider it an, as yet, undifferentiated aspect of the Object relation.

The expression of the Object develops out of the expression of Performative Objects, so it is hard to spot the earliest examples. The first examples we have for the two children illustrate the different forms an Object can take. The first example for Matthew is *ball,* an Object of his own action, which occurs relatively early. Nicky's first example is *fan,* which looks like a Volitional Object except that Nicky clearly wants a change of state of that Object. Thus, the action is external to Nicky. this more externalized form of Object occurs relatively late in Nicky's development.

Once again, Objects are first expressed in relation to situational context, later in relation to verbal context. Use in sequences followed use in isolation and preceded use in two-word sentences. Instruments and Locations of Agents have been treated as types of Objects because of their rarity in one-word speech.

Dative

Although the first examples of the Dative case occur relatively early, productivity is not arrived at until much later, and examples remain infrequent. This characteristic of the Dative case continues into two-word speech. The first examples for both boys correspond to the traditional notion of Dative, that is, the indirect object.

Nicky

For Nicky, the earliest instance of a Dative occurs during Nicky I—18(4) when, on two occasions he gives a book to his mother and says *mama.* Between 19(15) and 20(3), some examples occur in which the Dative is a body part. For instance, Nicky says *han(d)* when he wants his wet hands dried. When body parts were passively involved in action, they were considered to have the function of Dative because of their animacy. Similar examples occur during the formal session in the interval, Nicky III-19(29).

The first sequence involving a Dative occurs at Nicky sequence, although the Dative is more closely tied to the non-verbal context.

In this sequence *mama*, a Dative, encodes the animate recipient of an object from Nicky, the agent in the situation.

Nicky VI—22(21) represents the height of productivity of the Dative function in one-word form. The range of combinatorial possibilities of word and event is shown in Table 30. This Table includes the first instance of naming an animate Object of someone else's Action: Nicky says *(f)ishy* when Matthew has gone to feed the fish. During this same session, the first nonconversational sequence involving a Dative occurs: Nicky says *ban(ana)* followed by *teddy* when he gives a banana to his teddy bear.

Nicky VII—23(21) finds the first example of Dative clearly tied to verbal context, this time in isolated single-word form: Nicky's mother asks *What are you doing?* and Nicky, moving his foot up and down, responds *toes*.

At Nicky VIII—24(23), the Dative is incorporated into a number of different two-word utterances. One example, part of a complex sequence, involves negative Volition plus Dative: Nicky says *no feet* as Matthew puts his feet up on a stool.

Matthew

For Matthew, the first Dative occurs relatively early. At 11(28) he offers a bottle to his father and says *dada.* The first Datives to appear during a formal session occur at Matthew IV—16(2), when Matthew goes to his mother, hugs her and says *mommy.* During this same session, Matthew uses a Dative in response to verbal context as part of a partly imitative conversational sequence. His mother says *We're going byebye and get Lauren,* to which Matthew imitatively replies *bye*. At that point, his mother affirms *Yeah, byebye;* Matthew responds with *lala*, a Dative in relation to the verbal context.

Approximately 2 months later, there occur two examples of a benefactive type of Dative in which the beneficiary is removed from the situation in space and time: At 18(12), Matthew says *yaya* when he pours yoghurt in the kitchen and repeats it as he walks into the dining room to his sister Lauren. At 18(28), after Matthew's mother gives him a cracker, he reaches toward the cracker box saying *yaya*; when he gets another cracker, he proceeds into the dining room and offers it to his sister.

At 20(3), an interesting example occurs. His mother asks *Do you want to go with Mommy?* And he answers *daddy*. This is an example of a comitative Dative, one which also involves paradigmatic substitution.

The next development is the incorporation of the Dative into a multiword utterance. At 20(19), Matthew says *a cookie* upon seeing a cookie his mother was holding out of him. After taking it, he held out his other hand and said *Yaya a cookie*. In this example, the word *cookie* encodes an element which would have been communicated by the presence of the cookie at an earlier point in development. The situation is practically identical to situations reported two months earlier; the only change is that Matthew is now able to encode more elements of that situation. This example is particularly interesting because it shows a sequence of functions, viz. Dative, Object, which is rarely reported in the literature.

The first examples of Datives for both boys involve

handing something to a parent. Later developments involve expressing a benefactive goal and expressing animate objects. In Matthew's development, the benefactive examples essentially represent a Dative who is removed from the present situation.

There are relatively few examples of Datives, so it is hard to discuss their development in any detail. Nevertheless, the sequence of development is in general the same as that for other functions, from use in isolation to use in a verbal context, and from use in sequences to use in two-word sentences.

Object associated with another location

Expression of the function Associated Object involves naming one object in relation to another one. The object named may or may not be present in the situation. In the earliest examples, the associated entity is fairly close to the present situation. With age, however, both boys become capable of denoting metaphoric relations. this category of utterances is the semantic basis for attribution in mature speech.

10

Language Teaching Aids

The use of language teaching aids can be categorized according to various kinds of language teaching situations and different levels of teaching. Though some language teaching aids may be common in different kinds of language teaching situations but the purpose for their use varies according to situations. Language teaching aids are used by a teacher in imparting different skills of language. They are primarily used for making the language learning simple, effective and an interesting experience for the learner. Besides their essential use in teaching the basic language skills, they provide an effective medium for building the language environment into the classroom. The learners are able to observe and use the target language with the help of some of these aids more effectively. These aids are quite useful in explaining sociocultural contexts and cultural bound lexical items and concepts in a second language learning situation. Here we will briefly discuss the main characteristics of some of the very common language teaching aids.

The blackboard is considered as essential part of a classroom. There are different kinds of blackboards, but their function in language teaching is more or less the same. Besides its use in the introduction of new material, it can be used in the building of substitution tables, for writing short guided compositions and conversations etc. in collaboration with the class. Besides writing on the blackboard, at several occasions it is essential to draw simple lines, drawings and diagrams on it for explaining meaning or exact relationship between various lexical items and structures. A teacher must realize the value of the blackboard as a focus of interest for the entire class and must make the best use of this common and economical aid. Pictures and charts are also very useful and simple visual aids in presenting various situations essential for the language use. They can be used for teaching all linguistic features of the language. Various kinds of pictures like illustrations cut out from magazines, photographs, drawings, posters etc. can be prepared and selected by a teaching keeping in view their usefulness in teaching different linguistic features and cultural items.

Flash cards made of pieces of cardboard are also quite simple and useful visual aids. Various lexical items or sentences can be written or printed on these cards in bold letters. Flash cards may also present simple outline drownings of various objects like animals, birds, fruits, pieces of furniture etc. there cards can be used for various kinds of drills, exercises and tests. Similarly, maps and charts can also prove helpful visual aids in language teaching. They can be used for various kinds of drills and exercises in the classroom.

The use of dramatization, mime, gesture and facial expression etc. are also helpful aids in language teaching.

A teacher can involve his pupils in different kinds of roles and activities and use these as aids for imparting instructions in language skills. A language teacher has an important role to play as far as preparation, selection and the use of the above simple and common language teaching aids is concerned.

Various teaching aids have recently come into the use in the form of language laboratories, films, film projectors, film strips, film strip projectors synchronized with tape recorder, slides, slide projectors synchronised with tape recorder, closed circuit television, visphones and linguaphones, reading accelerators, tape recorders with taped lessons, microfilm readers and microfilms, microfische readers and microfische cards etc. Besides these aids, attempts have been made to use various types of programmed instruction such as "scrambled books', highly complex multi-channel teaching machines and 'response conductors' for language teaching. Atempts are being made to prepare programmed instruction courses in the forms of computer programmes.

Instruction through an electric classroom, which comprises of all the electronic and electro-mechanical gadgets listed above, may prove effective in the learning of the language, if it supplements the regular classroom instruction.

Among the available teaching aids, language laboratory is an important aid to language learning. Different types of language laboratories are currently being used. Main types of laboratories are: (a) Audio Passive (b) Audio Active (c) Audio Active Comparative and (d) Audio Active Comparative Controlled. Language laboratory facilitates a student to work at his own pace, select the materials of his own choice, hear the tape lesson distinctively without any sort of disturbance, and stop, rewind and replay the tape at his own choice. The students can practice their lessons without disturbing others. In short, the language laboratory as an aid in language teaching provides an opportunity and environment for practice in pronunciation, proper stress and intonation etc. by providing correct model for imitation; it reinforces the classroom work and saves the classroom time by providing different kinds of drills and exercises. The use of the language laboratory to the best advantage of the learner of the language largely depends on the nature and quality of the recorded materials, the degree to which materials supplement in the classroom work, the length and frequency of the laboratory periods and above all on the skill of the teacher who conducts the laboratory class. In case the recorded teaching materials do not supplement the classroom instruction and are technically inadequate, or, if the students are not monitored and correct by a trained teacher, the results will certainly be ineffective. The learning of language involves a great amount of exercise and drill work. The exercises and drills require a close supervision and frequent remedial correction by the skilled teacher, while monitoring the laboratory lessons.

For instance, drills given in language laboratory can provide an aural discrimination training to the learner in more effective way than in the class. In which the learner can recognise the phonemes of the language clearly and can discriminate the minimal pairs accurately. In vocal reproduction drills administered in the laboratory, the learner can the correct production of sounds in all possible combinations. A learner can utter words with correct stress and sentences with appropriate intonation in the language. Similarly, the drills may include the patterns for the construction of grammatical sentences in the language. It is needless to say that programming should be concerned with the imitation of the native pronunciation and intonation and with drilling structures and patterns which have first been introduced in the class.

The materials used for film and television courses must be assessed from the point of view of the contribution that they can make as the supplementary teaching materials in both the acquisition of language skills and to the understanding of the way of life of native speakers of the target language . Film and television have the capacity to present language and situation simultaneously, or, they present the language in a fully, contextualised form. This characteristic it shares with the classroom teacher. Films and television teaching programmes contribute to the teaching of language and culture simultaneously.

The use of audio-visual aids such slides, filmstrips, films and television courses make necessary for the language teacher to present their material at normal speed. The use of film and television in language teaching is still in its fancy.

It is import to keep in view some general principles regarding the use of language teaching aids. Each aid must make clear the purpose for which it is used in a particular language teaching situation. The aid must represent only one teaching point at a time. The purpose of the use of a particular teaching aid must be the focus of interest and not the aid itself.

11

Problems and Perspectives of Foreign Language Teaching

Foreign Language Departments have been started in the Universities and I.I.Ts with a special practical need. If the purpose of learning Foreign Languages is correctly formulated, it will help us to plan the curricula, to choose the teaching materials and the method of teaching. The great Russian scholar K.D. Ushinsky rightly said: "The purpose, with which we learn one or the other Foreign Language, is very important, because the purpose formulates the very method of learning. In order to formulate correctly the purpose of learning/teaching Foreign Language, one has to understand clearly the special nature of this subject.

Though there is a Department of Foreign Languages in almost every university and IIT, the nature of this subject greatly differs from other subjects taught in the other Departments. For example, by learning Physics or Chemistry, the students are taught the specific laws governing nature and are trained to use them in practical life. In the IITs and Universities the courses in Foreign Languages are not a regular branch of study. The Foreign

Languages such as French, German and Russian are taught only as a tool language for the post-graduates and research scholars who are studying other subjects such as Physics. Chemistry etc. The study of Foreign Language should give the learners the ability and skill to refer to the scientific and research journals in their field of study published in the Foreign Languages. Therefore, the study of a Foreign Language is more of practical nature than of academic pursuit. Acquiring a new means for receiving and transferring information may be the main idea of learning a Foreign Language in a Technical Institute or in any non-philological department. The main idea of teaching a Foreign Language in the Universities and IITs is to develop the necessary practical skill to handle the new language to acquire information in his/her field of study.

By practical skill it is understood here not only as speaking skill and understanding, as it is generally interpreted, but also as reading and writing. In the Technical Institutes and Universities the main attention in teaching Foreign Languages should be devoted to develop the skill to read, understand and translate simple technical texts. Therefore the teachers of Foreign Languages in the Technical Institute and Universities should take into account the students speciality not only for selecting the texts for reading, but also while developing the speaking, writing and understanding skill. Here, I like to underline the fact that first and foremost task is to develop the skill and ability to read, understand and translate popular science and technical texts rather than to develop speaking skill and reading of prose and poetry. Therefore, in the programme of study of Foreign Languages emphasis should be given to the former than to the latter aspect.

In the first year certificate course where the students are not yet trained to read original technical literature, reading and writing skill has to be developed using specially prepared texts on popular science or of general nature. At the level two specific requirements are made: (1) On the basis of the vocabulary and grammar taught, the students have to be trained to read and understand unknown texts without the help of a dictionary; and (2) the students are trained to read and understand the texts composed mainly of the grammatical material already taught and containing not more than 20% new words.

The ability to read and translate socio-political texts and popular science texts or prose and poetry is also equally important, which in general prepares the students to read and understand the texts on speciality, as any technical text is composed of general vocabulary and grammar. Any dictionary listing the minimum words required to read scientific texts shows that in the scientific or technical texts there are 80% words pertaining to general vocabulary. Therefore, it was proposed earlier that the reading skill had to be developed with and without dictionary.

The programme for the Foreign Language teaching in the universities and IITs, should consider the following aspects: Reading skill in its true sense of the word can be realised only when the reader automatically can perceive and understand greater part of the lexico-grammatical material contained in the text. If this is not possible, then reading turns out to be decoding the text, i.e. the teacher has to look into the dictionary almost every word. By training the students to read without using a dictionary, the students learn instantly to perceive and understand the language material to be learnt. Besides this in the process of such reading without translating the students learn to guess the meaning of the new words by context and on the basis of word building rules. Such an ability has to be developed among the students because this reduces the time required for looking into the dictionary. The curricula of the Foreign Language courses in the Universities and IITs have to be planned in such a way that one year study in the Foreign Language Department enables the students to acquire the basic skill necessary for reading and understanding simple texts of their speciality.

The second requirement is reading the texts containing not more than 15 to 20% new words with the help of dictionary. It is obvious that the students will come across new words, whose meanings they may not to able to guess by context. In such a case they have to refer to the dictionary. This second aspect trains the students to read complicated original scientific articles published in the Foreign Languages by suing the dictionary quickly and economically.

As it was mentioned earlier, the scope for the development of the speaking skill is limited. The important moment to be remembered in developing the speaking skill in a non-philological language department is to make a distinction between communicative skill and perceptible skill. These are two distinctive features in language learning. They have to be developed simultaneously. the communicative skill is developed by teaching simple conversations on a particular theme. It is better to choose the themes in consultation with the students—speciality and interest. the perspective skill is developed to understand the text while reading or understanding the spoken language. The Foreign Language teacher has to work in this line to develop both the communicative and perceptive skills of the learners simultaneously.

One of the most important methodological principles in Foreign Language teaching is to consider the mother-tongue of the learners. It is enough to say that the famous American linguist N. Chomsky pointed out that 'the pedagogical grammar' i.e. the grammar meant for learning a language by the foreigners should be based on the linguistic grammar which takes into account the similarity and difference between the foreign language and mother-tongue. Investigations carried out in Soviet Union and abroad show that the specific peculiarities of the Foreign Language when compared with the mother-tongue are the major source of difficulties. Besides that different mother tongues may pose different difficulties in learning one or the other Foreign Language. Therefore, in order to give the correct explanation for grammatical category, to select correctly the types of exercises and their quantum it is essential to know the difficulties which may be cropping up while learning a given grammatical or phonemic phenomenon and this in its turn expects the teacher to compare this phenomenon with its equivalent in the mother-tongue and prognosticate the probably difficulties. This is the basic principle to be observed in taking the help of mother-tongue while teaching a Foreign Language.

Learning a Foreign Language in the Universities and IITs is not compulsory and the Foreign Language courses are not very popular either in India. the main reason for the unpopularity of the courses is that the learners are not very sure whether they will be able to acquire enough command over the language, as it is only an optional subject and taught as part-time courses. Secondly, the students often do not have any idea, how they are going to use this knowledge in their future work. the knowledge which the students acquire while studying their main subjects are applied into practice in their work or in every day activity. As far as the Foreign Languages are concerned, it seems to them that there is very little practical utility in learning a Foreign Language. This type of pessimistic approach on the part of the student is understandable, because in India Foreign Language teaching is treated as a separate discipline, as if it has nothing to do with the students' curricula. This, in my opinion, is the result of not understanding the specific nature of Foreign Language as an academic subject, hose role is to serve as a tool language to acquire, disseminate and provide scientific information. Because of this specific nature, Foreign Languages specially have greater possibilities of practical application.

In this connection, there is another important aspect while planning the curricula for the teaching of Foreign Language in the Universities and IITs. The teacher of Foreign Languages, who teaches this subject as an optional subject, should work in collaboration and consultation with the teachers of the major disciplines offered in one universities and IITs, with whose help the Foreign Language Teacher should choose the theme for conversation and additional texts for translation. Such an experiment will provide greater perspectives in the field of Foreign Language Teaching. By translating the article from the modern scientific and technical journals, the students feel the practical advantage of knowing the Foreign Language in acquiring and using the most modern scientific information in his work. In this way the students begin to feel himself as an independent researcher and takes greater interest in the language. The appropriate skill to handle the Foreign Language enables the students to widen the horizon of his subject knowledge. Therefore, the success in organising this optional course depends not only on the Foreign Language Teacher, but greatly depends on the students and the teachers of Foreign Language have to work in co-operation with the other teachers of the subjects. It is not possible for the Foreign Language teachers to have contact with the students of the other faculties and, therefore, it is not possible to explain to the students the advantages in learning one or the other Foreign Language. The Foreign Language teacher at the most can keep up the enthusiasm and tempo with which the students came to the department of Foreign Language to learn a new means to acquire scientific knowledge.

As these courses are only optional, the leading factor of this course has to be of voluntary nature. This principal has to be observed not only at the time of organising the course but also throughout the duration of the course. While answering the questions or evaluating the progress made by the students by conducting tests, there should not be any amount of compulsion on the part of the teachers. It is better to avoid giving marks in evaluating the progress made by the students. the progress can be assessed orally by giving grades A.B.C. For the purpose of documentation, if at all it is required to do so, individual marks can be awarded at the end of the course or at the end of the semester.

During the first year it is necessary to use the appropriate methodological recommendations, audio-visual aids and other means which will kindle the intelligence of the learners. The teaching material has to be carefully chosen. The teacher has to choose the type of assignments which will give maximum results in activising the language abilities. Here the teacher has the liberty to use pictures, slides, special films to develop the speaking skill.

During the second year of the course greater part of the time is spent in reading literature pertaining to one's speciality. Simultaneously spoken skill is also developed by discussing over the themes which are provided in the programme. Sometimes popular science texts or even prose may kindle the interest of the students to develop their skill. This has to be decided by the teacher taking into account the individual's interest and tests.

During the second year independent tasks can be assigned to the students. Here the students may be asked to read and translate an article pertaining to his field of study. Besides the regular classes, the teacher has to plan individual consultations to help the students in fulfilling the individual assignments. Such consultations can be arranged once in a week. At the end of the year it may be advisable to give independent assignments to be fulfilled at home with in a particular span of time. This may serve the purpose of evaluating the progress made by the student. This assignment has to the chosen again, keeping in view the students' interest and tests.

Some methodological issues in investigating learner language

In the previous chapters, we have examined issues related to the investigation of what the learner knows about the language. While we have been looking at different components of the learner's communicative competence the procedures we have used to evaluate these different components have shared certain similarities. In this chapter, we focus upon methodological issues to be considered in constructing needs analysis instruments.

A number of identifiable factors must be considered in evaluating a learner's abilities in the second language. These factors break down, we believe, into those relating to the identity of the addressee, the topic of the discourse, and the procedures required by the task itself.

The addressee

In any situation involving communicative interaction, the second language learner will not simply be speaking in a vacuum—there will inevitably be someone to speak to. If an elicitation task intended to foster communicative use of the language is developed for the classroom, then it must provide an addressee who has some reason for listening to the speaker. Recognizing the importance of the addressee must also involve a recognition of the effect which the identity and role of the addressee can have on what the speaker says. In some circumstances, the grammatical forms used by the speaker may be strongly influenced by the particular addressee involved.

According to Speech Accommodation theorists like Bell and Giles, the learner shifts styles in response to his perception of the addressee, either attempting to *converge*, making his productions more congruent with those of the person addressed, or to *diverge*, making productions congruent with those of some other group of speakers. Thus, for example, a learner speaking to a teacher of the target language might be *expected* to produce language forms which are more grammatically accurate than when speaking to another learner from his own country. On the other hand, some learners have been observed at times to produce forms with *less* grammatical accuracy when speaking to the teacher. A good example is Rampton's observation, that ungrammatical constructions used by students seemed to be the students' way of stressing, for the teacher's also by systematically varied in an attempt to determine whether, and how, these factors affect variable language forms.

The task

We have argued, for a 'task-based' methodology to be used in the investigation of learners' communicative competence. Such a methodology, described in detail in Brown and Yule and elsewhere, provides a speaker with: (1) some pre-selected information to convey; (2) a listener who requires that information in order to complete a task, and (3) the awareness that an information gap exists. These three criteria are, we have argued, crucial for any elicitation task which is to provide the investigator with both spontaneous and, at the same time, controlled data.

In fact, we find a wide variety of tasks in use to gather data on learners' formal accuracy, and sociolinguistic and strategic skills in the second language classroom. Examples are tasks rating the grammaticality of target language sentences, correcting target language sentences with errors in them, reading minimal pairs and word lists, answering questionnaires, telling stories in response to tightly controlled visual stimuli, role plays, and responding to questions like 'Tell me what you did last summer?' In addition to the problem of maintaining topic constant, which we have just discussed, there are other task factors which vary greatly even in the brief list we have just provided, any of which may have an effect upon the formal accuracy, level of appropriateness, or communicative effectiveness of the learners' language.

The first point to consider is that these different tasks elicit different tasks elicit different amounts of discourse—

from single sentences to long monologues. On grammaticality judgment tasks, learners may not produce language at all, but rather read sentences and judge their correctness or conformity to some implied target-language norm. Some grammaticality judgment tasks may ask learners to rewrite or correct sentences which are incorrect, but often these rewritings may consist only of a word or two. Can accuracy scores on these tasks really be compared to accuracy scores on tasks where the subjects are asked to produce extended discourse in the second language? In addition to differences in sheer volume of data produced on these different tasks, the amount of conectedness of the discourse may vary considerably, from single, unconnected sentences to long, extended pieces of connected prose.

Second, the mode of discourse may vary, from descriptions and instructions to narration and persuasion. In the example cited above, the topic of 'summer holidays' could easily have led one learner to *describe* his garden, another to *complain* about her summer job, and yet another to *narrate* a close brush with death—thereby eliciting different discourse modes from different learners. and the language forms which we have selected to study may occur with different degrees of frequency in different types of discourse. For example, past tense forms are not likely to occur in the description of an apparatus. However, they are more likely to occur in narratives. Furthermore, as we have already seen, there is research evidence that different modes of discourse place different demands upon the language system, so that a learner may find it easier to be grammatically accurate within one discourse type than in another. Using carefully designed elicitation prompts will go a long way towards controlling discourse mode. The elicitation materials provided of this book are designed to elicit extended, connected discourse on predetermined topics, and to control the discourse mode produced by the learner.

Note that it is not enough for teachers to select a picture at random, show it to the students, and ask them to describe it. Such a procedure may not be much more effective at controlling topic and discourse mode than 'Tell me what you did during your summer holiday'.

1. The prompts themselves must be carefully chosen to elicit a particular topic and not others. In observing an ESL class recently, we watched a student teacher run into difficulties because the picture prompt she had chosen contained a number of distracting elements. She had wanted a picture of a tennis shoe. But the prompt she chose showed a six-foot tall tennis shoe standing in a living room, surrounded by a number of astonished people. 'Just talk about the shoe,' the teacher said. But her students had a great deal of difficulty determining exactly what topic they were expected to comment upon simply because the prompt was poorly chosen.

2. The instructions given the learners will be crucial in narrowing the range of topics and the mode of discourse to be used with them. For example, if teachers would like the learners to give directions on how to assemble a piece of equipment shown in a series of pictures, they will have to word their instructions very carefully to ensure that their students do not simply *describe* each picture instead of providing directions for assembly.

3. Another aspect of the instructions should be kept in mind: a learner may be told to be careful to be grammatically accurate, or may be told that grammatical accuracy is unimportant. While the identity of the addressee and other factors such as setting may affect the learners' willingness to follow such instructions, we must assume that differing instructions may have different effects upon the language forms produced.

4. Another factor has to do with the amount of time allotted for the task. the accuracy with which learners produce certain language forms seems to vary systematically in relation to the amount of time they have to perform the task. Clearly, this factor of time must be related to the question of medium: writing typically allows one more time than speaking for modification of language form.

5. Ultimately, of course, teachers should try the prompts and instructions out on one or two native speakers before using them with their classes, in order to ensure that these do in fact effectively limit topic and control discourse mode in the way they would like.

Each of the three major features of the elicitation task: identity of addressee, topic, and task design, should be kept in mind in investigating grammatical accuracy, sociolinguistic appropriateness, and communicative effectiveness. The interest instructor, over a period of time, might vary some of these features to determine their effect upon the communicative behavior of particular groups of learners. For example, learners might be asked to perform the same tasks but with different addresses, and their language examined for variation under these different conditions. Or, the identity of the addressee and the other factors might be held constant, and only the operations required by the task changed.

The data analysis

In addition to deciding what sort of elicitation task to provide, one must decide how the data are to be analyzed.

The first point to be made here relates to the use of 'obligatory context' which has typically been used to analyze the occurrence of a target language form in 'natural' language data—that is, extended discourse over which the learner has had some control. Briefly, an 'obligatory context' for any language form is a linguistic context in which native speakers of the target language would be obliged to supply that language form in order to produce a grammatically correct utterance. An example might be:

Yesterday John hik—up to Seven Lakes Basin.

Here, an 'obligatory context' for a past tense morpheme -*ed* is created. For any learner, the number of obligatory contexts for any target language form may be countered up, and the number of times the form was supplied in such obligatory contexts may be calculated.

There are many problems with the use of obligatory context in analyzing the occurrence of forms in natural discourse. It seems increasingly clear, for example, that many learners are quite adept at avoiding the production of some obligatory contexts for problematic target language forms. This will mean that one learner may have produced all the linguistic contexts of interest in large numbers, and another learner may not have produced any of one particular linguistic context. This will present massive problems for analysis, in comparing one learner with another. Another problem is that analysis by means of occurrence in obligatory context does not permit the analyst to identify cases of overgeneralization in the data—that is, cases where the target form was supplied in contexts *other* than the obligatory contexts. For example, the *-ed* marker might be observed to occur in all the obligatory contexts for the past tense marker—but the learner's hundred per cent accuracy in obligatory context may not mean that the form has been acquired; *-ed* may also occur *whenever* a verb is used by the learner, in contexts where no native speaker would use such a marker, as in 'You should walked.' Analysis in terms of the obligatory context would be unable to capture this pattern in the data. Alternative methods of analysis which allow one to identify cases of overgeneralization are needed and have been proposed by a variety of researchers, and should be drawn upon when we analyze our data.

The second point to be made here has been alluded to earlier, and this is the importance of establishing good baseline data for the purposes of comparison. There are two components involved in establishing a baseline: first, the *essential structure* of the task must be established, and second, data must be obtained from native speakers. The establishment of the essential structure of the task involves determining which persons and objects are mentioned by all, or almost all, the subjects in completing the task. Establishing the essential structure allows the teacher to then objectively evaluate the communicative effectiveness of individual students. In relation to the second component—native speaker data—far too often, classroom elicitation measures are given only to second language learners; teachers then go on to analyze the learners' performance and to suggest causes for this performance by comparing it with hypothesized productions of some 'ideal' native speaker of the target language. The point here is that real learner performance data are being compared to some idealized concept of native speakers' use of the target language, and *not* to real performance on the same tasks by speakers of the target language. Of course, for practical reasons classroom teachers must often rely on their own intuition in judging learner performance; it is not possible to norm *all* elicitation measures on native speakers. However, often a 'quick-and dirty' check with even *one* native speaker can be very informative.

In a recent study which attempted to elicit production of direct object pronouns on several tasks, second language learners were asked to describe a series of pictures which were supposed to force production of direct object pronouns in referring over and over to the same entity. The learners, however, did not use direct object pronouns much; rather, they usually repeated the full noun phrase:

The boy sees a ball, and he picks up the ball, and throws the ball, and he sits on the ball, and he puts the ball in a mailbox.

Since the native language of these subjects did not require direct object pronouns, but rather allowed zero anaphora, initially it was thought that native language transfer might indirectly be causing some 'hyper-correct' behavior, since of course everyone *knows* that native speakers of English would not produce such a stilted piece of discourse. Fortunately, one native speaker of English was asked to perform the same task—and the same pattern occurred; probably something in the design of the task itself elicited the repetition of full noun phrases. In order to make valid interpretations of the patterns in our data, then, we need to ask native speakers of the target language to perform the same tasks which the learners perform, in order to establish a valid target baseline.

Finally, in analyzing the performance of second language learners on productive tasks, a very detailed examination of the data may be quite useful. For example, Lund who was studying learner accuracy on verb forms, listed the particular verbs used by individual learners in narrating the same story. He discovered that Learner A, who had a high formal accuracy rate overall, also seemed to have told the story using very few verbs, and all of these had simple conjugations, while Learner B, who had a lower overall formal accuracy rate on this task, had told the story using a wider variety of verbs, many of them requiring difficult conjugations. Our conclusions about the proficiency of these two learners, and the causes of their variability in formal accuracy on this task, may be tempered by such a detailed qualitative analysis.

We hope that the methodological issues which we have raised will be of help to classroom teachers interested in improving their investigation of their learners' communicative competence, as outside observers looking in upon the learner. In Part Four we attempt to explore the learner's abilities from the inside looking out—that is, the learner's perception of his or her own abilities.

Analysis of the data

To study the interrelationships of the various language skills, correlation, terminal status, and the significance of the differences between consecutively tested age levels are used. Product-moment correlations between the several variables have been determined for the total subsamples at each age level. The N used in computing all correlations presented in this chapter is 60. No correlations are reported for the separate sex or SES groups. With an N of 60 an r above .30 is significant at the .01 level, and an r of .21 satisfied the .05 level of confidence.

Terminals status measures are presented for each major language area tested. Consistent with the earlier chapters, the terminal status scores are presented for boys and girls, USES and LSES groups, and for total subsamples. The terminal status score, like any percentage, depends for stability upon the size of the sample and the magnitude of the raw scores being considered. In this study, the N at each age level varies from 18for the USES group to 30 for the boys and girls to 42 for the LSES groups to 60 for the total subsample. The range of raw scores varies considerably, but for these major measures is always substantial.

For each major language measure, the mean score of the subjects at the oldest age tested is taken as a measure of terminal status and the percentage of this score attained by each younger age group is calculated. With the scores of the 8-year-old subjects taken as a measure of terminal status, comparisons are made of the development of articulation, sentence structure, sound discrimination as measured in paired nonsense syllables, and vocabulary as measured by the Seashore-Eckerson English Recognition Vocabulary Test. The scores of the 5-year-old subjects were taken as a measure of terminal status when a different test of any language area was used with the preschool and the school-age subjects. These include sound discrimination and vocabulary. Although different tests were used to measure articulation at the preschool and the school ages, terminal status scores were not taken at both 5 and 8 years since the same sounds were measured throughout the age range.

Throughout this monograph reference has been made to the significance of the differences between consecutively tested age subsamples. These are brought together for the major measures in this chapter.

Correlation analysis

In Table 1 the intercorrelations among the various language skills are presented separately for each age subsample. In interpreting them it must be remembered that different measures of intelligence, sound discrimination, and vocabulary are used at the preschool and at the school ages. At 6, 7, 8 years of age the IQ is based most frequently on the Stanford-binet which was administered by kindergarten teachers. The IQ-equivalent is the only measured approximation of intelligence at the preschool level. The correlations with IQ-equivalent are presented in Table 1 under the heading "Ammons Vocabulary" since the scores are based upon that test.

Of the 189 correlations presented, 76 per cent are significant at the .01 level and only 12 per cent do not reach the .05 level of confidence. The magnitude of the intercorrelations varies with the language areas tested, the particular test used, and the age of the subsample being considered. The highest correlations are found between sound discrimination and sound discrimination vocabulary. At each of the preschool ages tested the r's are about .90. The intercorrelations among the measures related to sentence structure are only slightly lower. Of the 24 correlations reported among the length of remark, the

Table 1. Product-moment correlations among major measures by age

	CA							
Measure	3	3.5	4	4.5	5	6	7	8
Total articulation versus:								
Sound discrimination	59	.42	.58	.41	.44	.67	.69	.47
Length of remark	62	.47	.27	.26	.52	.45	.23	.18
Complexity of remark	.66	.57	.30	.49	.35	.46	.08	.15
Number of different words	.65	.53	.41	.34	.62	.34	.24	.19
Ammons vocabulary	.47	.48	.24	.41	.27			
Sound discrimination								
Vocabulary	.54	.42	.52	.42	.42			
Corrected basic vocabulary						.34	.45	.40
Uncorrected basic vocabulary						.39	.46	.38
Intelligence quotient						.37	.39	.29
Sound discrimination versus:								
Length of remark	.45	.23	.32	.40	.69	.40	.36	.01
Complexity of remark	.49	.25	.40	.37	.50	.41	.25	.05
Number of different words	.49	.44	.45	.49	.54	.26	.37	.02
Sound discrimination								
Vocabulary	.93	.95	.94	.91	.96			
Corrected basic vocabulary						.44	.46	.58
Uncorrected basic vocabulary						.51	.49	.52
Intelligence quotient						.54	.47	.45
Length of remark versus:								
Complexity of remark	.89	.81	.88	.90	.59	.91	.68	.77
Number of different words	.91	.85	.93	.89	.91	.84	.68	.80

Ammons vocabulary	.55	.26	.24	.52	.26			
Sound discrimination vocabulary	.42	.21	.27	.54	.61			
Corrected basic vocabulary						.32	.16	.06
Uncorrected basic vocabulary						.39	.16	.06
Intelligence quotient						.39	.08	.15
Complexity of remark versus:								
Number of different words	.87	.77	.69	.76	.80	.82	.52	.68
Ammons vocabulary	.54	.29	.30	.46	.31			
Sound discrimination vocabulary	.45	.28	.31	.33	.43			
Corrected basic vocabulary						.29	.18	.12
Uncorrected basic vocabulary						.36	-.03	.13
Intelligence quotient						.26	.00	.30
Number of different words versus:								
Ammons vocabulary	.57	.40	.56	.57	.49			
Sound discrimination Vocabulary	.45	.37	.39	.47	.27			
Corrected basic vocabulary	.22	.31	.17					
Uncorrected basic vocabulary						.28	.31	.19
Intelligence quotient						.26	.28	.22
Ammons vocabulary versus:								
Sound discrimination	.51	.66	.42	.46	.36			
Corrected basic vocabulary versus:						.91	.94	.91
Intelligence quotient						.50	.57	.56
Uncorrected basic vocabulary versus:								
Intelligence quotient						.50	.55	.64

complexity of remark, and the number of different words used, only 6 fall between .5 and .7, while 18 are above .75. This is not unexpected since these three sentence variables would seem necessarily to be intimately dependent upon one another. Although there is considerable variability in the magnitude of the correlations between the several vocabulary measures and other language variables, they are generally in a lower range. Of the 70 correlations among these variables, only one reaches .6. The mean correlation reported for the Ammons vocabulary test and both the Seashore-Eckerson scores is somewhere between .3 and .4.

Although no marked age trends are evident, some differences are apparent in the magnitude of the correlations at different ages. For those language areas in which the same test was used over the age span covered in this study, essentially no age trends are found in the inter-correlations among length of response, complexity of response, and number of different words used. The size of the correlations among these sentence variables is substantial throughout the age range. The correlations between these measures and total articulation score tend to decrease slightly with age. This decrease in the relationship of sentence variables with articulation may be spurious, resulting from the large number of maximum scores attained at the older ages. However, it may be a true reflection of language growth in the earlier years. At this time when the variation in articulatory skill among children of the same age is greater, articulation may actually be more closely related to talkativeness, size of vocabulary, and the use of complex grammatical expressions.

Schneiderman does not report correlations between articulation and her combined language score. However, when her subjects were divided into upper, middle, and lower groups on the basis of the magnitude of this score, the differences in the mean articulation scores obtained by the three groups were statistically significant. When the subjects in these groups were matched on MA and CA, the differences among their articulation scores were no longer differentiated significantly as the F was reduced to 2.0. In both analyses the trend in the articulation scores was the same: the group receiving the highest combined language score made the fewest articulation errors, the middle, group made slightly more such errors, and the lowest group made the most articulation errors.

Since different tests were used to measure sound discrimination and vocabulary at the preschool and the school ages, terminal status measures for these language skills are taken at both 5 and 8 years. For sound discrimination the trends in the size of the correlations differ for the two. From 3 to 5 there is essentially no trend in the size of the correlations between sound discrimination and the length of response, the complexity of response, the number of different words used, and the total articulation score. From 6 to 8 years, however, there is a tendency for all the correlations between sound discrimination and these language variables to decrease with age. Although this decrease is somewhat irregular, it is still apparent at the oldest ages tested. This may be in part a function of the reduction in SD as the ceiling of the sound discrimination test is approached. Because of this it would have been of value to extend these measures to older age levels.

For the subsamples from 3 to 5 years, the correlations of both sound discrimination score and sound discrimination vocabulary with the various language variables are quite similar. Over the entire age range the correlations between total articulation and sound discrimination scores decrease slightly. Correlations between the various language variables and sound discrimination vocabulary at the preschool age also decrease slightly as age is increased. At the younger ages a difference is found in the magnitude of the correlations between the Ammons vocabulary score and both sound discrimination score and sound discrimination vocabulary. From 3 to 5 years the correlations between the Ammons vocabulary scores and sound discrimination decrease, while those with sound discrimination vocabulary do not vary with age. From 6 to 8 years the correlations between sound discrimination and the Seashore-Eckerson vocabulary scores do not vary regularly with age, while those between sound discrimination and IQ decrease slightly, although they are not markedly related to age. The correlations with the Ammons scores and the other language variables at the preschool ages resemble trends found at the older ages in correlations with IQ more than those found with other vocabulary measures.

Vocabulary is another of the language areas in which different tests are used in measurement. During the preschool years the correlations between Amons vocabulary and sound discrimination scores decrease with age. At this period all other correlations with either the Ammons vocabulary scores or the sound discrimination vocabulary show no real age trends. From 6 to 8 years the correlations between the corrected and uncorrected Seashore-Eckerson basic vocabulary scores also bear little relation to age. During the early school years there is a tendency for the magnitude of the correlations between vocabulary and length and complexity of response to decrease some with age. the number of different words used in the responses may be looked upon as a measure of vocabulary of use. With this vocabulary measure a decrease in correlations is noted with articulation and sound discrimination, but there is little relation to age with both length and complexity of remark.

The decrease in the magnitude of these correlations at the older ages may indicate that at these ages the samples of language obtained in spontaneous utterances in a child-adult setting are not long enough for the complexities of sentence structure and the larger vocabulary of use to become apparent. Schneiderman has reported a correlation of .17 between sentence length and vocabulary with 6-to-7year-old children. This is considerably lower than the .32 and .39 found with the Seashore-Eckerson test at 6 years in the present study, but it is in close agreement with the correlations of .16 and .19 reported at 7 years.

There is no consistent trend in the relationships between the measures of intelligence and the various language variables over the age range studied. For the 6-to-8-year-old subjects only the correlations of IQ with sound discrimination and two Seashore-Eckerson basic vocabulary scores reach any substantial magnitude. No comparisons can be made with a similar vocabulary measure at the preschool ages. The relation between IQ and sound discrimination increases slightly, which contrasts with the relation found during the preschool years. The correlations between IQ and articulation are substantial, dropping only at the highest CA tested.

During the school years there is a tendency for the relationships of the three measures of sentence development with IQ-equivalent to decrease. During the preschool years the size of the correlations tends to be unstable, particularly in the early years. This may reflect the inadequacy of the intellectual measure or the inadequacy of the sample of speech obtained in the utterances of the youngsters. It is probably the latter. Reasonably it is expected that intelligence is related to the length and complexity of sentence and to the number of different words a child uses. To determine the really meaningful relations which probably obtain among these variables, longer samples of speech are needed at the older ages included in this study.

Agreement with the findings of Schneiderman is close on two of the three possible comparisons of correlations between language variables and intelligence which can be made. She reports an r of—.35 between articulation score and MA for 6-to-7 year-olds. The IQ obtained on a restricted age of two months in the present study may be considered an intellectual unit comparable to the MA over a wider age range. In the present study the r between IQ and articulation score for 7-year-olds is .37 and for 7-year-olds it is .39. Since the articulation score used by Schneiderman is an error score and that used in the present study is a measure of correct articulation, these three correlations are nearly identical. This close agreement exists in spite of the fact that a verbal test was used in the present study to measure intelligence while Schneiderman used a nonverbal test.

The correlation of .48 reported by Schneiderman between vocabulary and MA is essentially equal to the .50 found at 6 years with both the corrected and uncorrected basic Seashore-Eckerson vocabulary scores and width the .55 and .57 found at 7 years in the present study. Schneiderman reports a correlation of —.003 between MA and sentence length whereas the comparable correlations in the present study are .39 and .08 at 6 and 7 years respectively. This difference could be accounted for partially by the use of verbal and nonverbal intelligence tests. It is more likely, however, that the relative adequacy of the samples of verbalizations is the more important factor. In the present study the relationship between sentence length and IQ-equivalent is considerably higher at the preschool ages. This, may indicate that the size of the sample of verbalization at these ages is sufficiently large to include more adequately the range of variations in the complexity of sentence structure which is likely to occur.

The intercorrelations among the language variables are presented in Table 2 with intelligence partialled out. For the subsamples from 3 to 5 the Ammons scores are partialled out; for the subsamples from 6 to 8 the Stanford-Binet IQ's are partialed out. The magnitude of all of these correlations is substantial. Essentially the same intercorrelations are highest, middle, or lowest as found for the zero-order correlations. The correlations between sound discrimination and sound discrimination vocabulary are still highest and range in the .90's. Those among the length of response, the complexity of response, and the number of different words are next high.

The trends with age in the magnitude of the correlations are essentially similar to those evident in Table 1. The correlations of sound discrimination with length of response, complexity of response, and number of different words vary irregularly. This is more evident at the older age than at the younger ages, and particularly in correlations with articulation and sound discrimination.

In Table3 the zero- and first-order intercorrelations reported by Williams on 3-to-4-year-old children are compared with the comparable correlations on 3.5-year-

Table 2. Product-moment correlations among major measures by age with intelligence partialled out

Measure	CA 3	3.5	4	4.5	5	6	7	8
Total articulation versus:								
Sound discrimination	.53	.42	.34	.14	.58	.27	.15	.14
Length or remark	.44	.41	.35	.06	.48	.36	.22	.14
Complexity of remark	.55	.51	.25	.37	.30	.40	.09	.07
Number of different words	.53	.42	.34	.14	.58	.27	.15	.14
Sound discrimination								
Vocabulary	.45	.18	.48	.44	.41			
Corrected basic vocabulary						.19	.30	.30
Uncorrected basic vocabulary						.26	.32	.26
Sound discrimination versus:								
Length of remark	.32	.09	.24	.45	.69	.24	.37	-.06
Complexity of remark	.37	.09	.31	.39	.50	.33	.28	-.10
Number of different words	.37	.26	.25	.57	.57	.15	.28	-.09
Sound discrimination								
vocabulary	.93	.92	.93	.99	.99			
Corrected basic vocabulary						.23	.27	.44
Uncorrected basic vocabulary						.33	.31	.34
Length of remark versus:								
Complexity of remark	.84	.79	.87	.84	.56	.91	.68	.71
Number of different words	.87	.84	.99	.85	.93	.83	.99	.81
Sound discrimination								
vocabulary	.38	.12	.16	.37	.18			
Corrected basic vocabulary						.16	.14	-.03
Uncorrected basic vocabulary						.24	.18	-.09
Complexity of remark versus:								
Number of different words	.82	.75	.66	.68	.78	.81	.52	.66

Sound discrimination								
vocabulary	.24	.12	.21	.15	.37			
Corrected basic vocabulary						.19	-.22	-.07
Uncorrected basic vocabulary						.27	.03	.09
Number of different words versus:								
Sound discrimination								
vocabulary	.22	.15	.21	.28	.12			
Corrected basic								
vocabulary.						.11	.18	.06
Uncorrected basic vocabulary						.18	.19	.06
Corrected basic vocabulary versus:						.18	.19	.06
Corrected basic vocabulary versus:								
Uncorrected basic vocabulary						.89	.91	.87

old subjects in the present study. The particular intelligence test upon which Williams obtained the MA used in his computations is not reported. Although several comparable language areas are measured by Williams and by the author, only in the classification of the complexity of the verbal expressions of the children was the technique used in the two studies identical. If the number of different words used in the verbal expressions is taken as a rough measure of vocabulary of use, there is little agreement in the correlations between the several measures of vocabulary and the other measures either within or between the Templin and Williams studies. The agreement in the correlations between IQ and IQ-equivalent are somewhat closer. The problem of the real relation of these variables to intelligence is not adequately faced at the 3-to-4-year levels since comparable measures are not available. the divergence in the results also emphasizes the fact that vocabulary is not a unit characteristic; there are different vocabularies which need to be studied and identified.

The agreement of the intercorrelations among articulation, length of response, and complexity of response as reported by the author and by Williams is high when the zero-order correlations are considered, but lower when intelligence is partialled out. The agreement among these correlations may be much closer than is apparent in this comparison. The differences in the magnitude of correlations with the various vocabulary measures are related to the basic question of adequate vocabulary measurement. This is an area which needs further investigation. The differences in the relationship with intelligence are probably tied up with the measure of intelligence used. The IQ-equivalent used in this study behaves somewhat more like a measure of vocabulary than intelligence. Some of the observed differences in the two studies are probably merely a reflection of the variation in size of samples.

Terminal status analysis

The Ammons Full-Range Picture Vocabulary Test and the sound discrimination vocabulary test were given only to preschool children. Different sound discrimination measures were given to the preschool and the school-age children. On these three measures the achievement of the 6-year-old subsamples is taken as a measure of terminal status. Direct comparisons cannot be made with those measures in which the scores attained by 8-year-old subjects were taken as a measure of terminal status.

Of the three measures in which the scores of the 5-year-old subsamples were taken as a measure of terminal status, the sound discrimination vocabulary shows the least growth over the two-year span. There is a increment of only about 20 percent. For both the Ammons vocabulary test and the sound discrimination test the increment over this same period is approximately 40 per cent. The 3-year-olds have achieved about 60 per cent of the attainment of the 5-year-olds in these language areas. This is within the range of percentages obtained on the other major language measures when the scores of the 5-year-olds were taken as a terminal status measure. In total articulation and complexity of response, for example, the 3-year-old subsample attains about 60 per cent of the score of the 5-year-olds. The mean number of different words used in the responses, the total number of words used, and the mean length of the five longest responses of the 3-year-olds are about at 70 per cent of the attainment of the 5-year-olds. this increment of about 30 per cent over these two years indicates that skill in these language variables is increasing more rapidly than in sound discrimination vocabulary but less rapidly than in total articulation, complexity of utterance, and Ammons vocabulary score.

Comparisons made at the 3-year level show that at this age less than 50 per cent of the achievement of the 8-year-olds has been attained in articulation, length of responses, and the number of different words; about 40 per cent of the degree of complexity of sentences; and about 20 per cent of the use of subordination.

While the Seashore-Eckerson tests were given only to 6- 7-, and 8-year-olds the comparisons at these ages can be made with any measure taken as a measure of terminal status. At least 85 percent of the achievement of the 8-year-old subsamples is attained by 6-year-olds on all language measures except the two basic scores on the Seashore-Eckerson vocabulary test. For these, approximately 50 per cent of the growth achieved by 8 years occurs between 6 and 8. Other investigators have reported substantial maturity in language in the early school years, but continued growth in vocabulary until well into adulthood. Since deceleration in growth usually occurs as maximum performance is being reached, the finding of proportionately more vocabulary increment in the early school years is in keeping with the findings of other investigators.

The scores of the 8-year-old boys are not taken as measures of terminal status since the scores of the two sexes are not sufficiently different to justify such separate consideration. On all variables except subordination and sound discrimination the 3-year-old boys achieve from 1.0 to 11.2 per cent more of the score of the 8-year-old girls than o 3-year-old girls. At this age the mean achievement of the boys is 4 percentage points higher than that of the girls. However, this acceleration for the boys does not hold throughout the age range studied. On the whole, 8-year-old boys attain slightly higher scores than girls on only three of the measures: Seashore-Eckerson vocabulary scores, use of subordination, and total articulation. On the latter the boys at 7 years about equal the attainment of the 6-year-old girls. In the other two areas, the boys are somewhat superior to the girls throughout the age range. On all the other language variables reported in Table 67 the achievement of boys and girls is about equal at 8 years of age. For several preceding test intervals, boys tend to receive scores about equal to those of girls one test interval younger.

The achievement of the 3-year-old LSES group on all measures reported here is lower than that for the USES group at this same age. The differences between the 3-year-old USES and LSES groups range from 1.9 to 12.4 percentage points with a mean difference of 7.1 points.

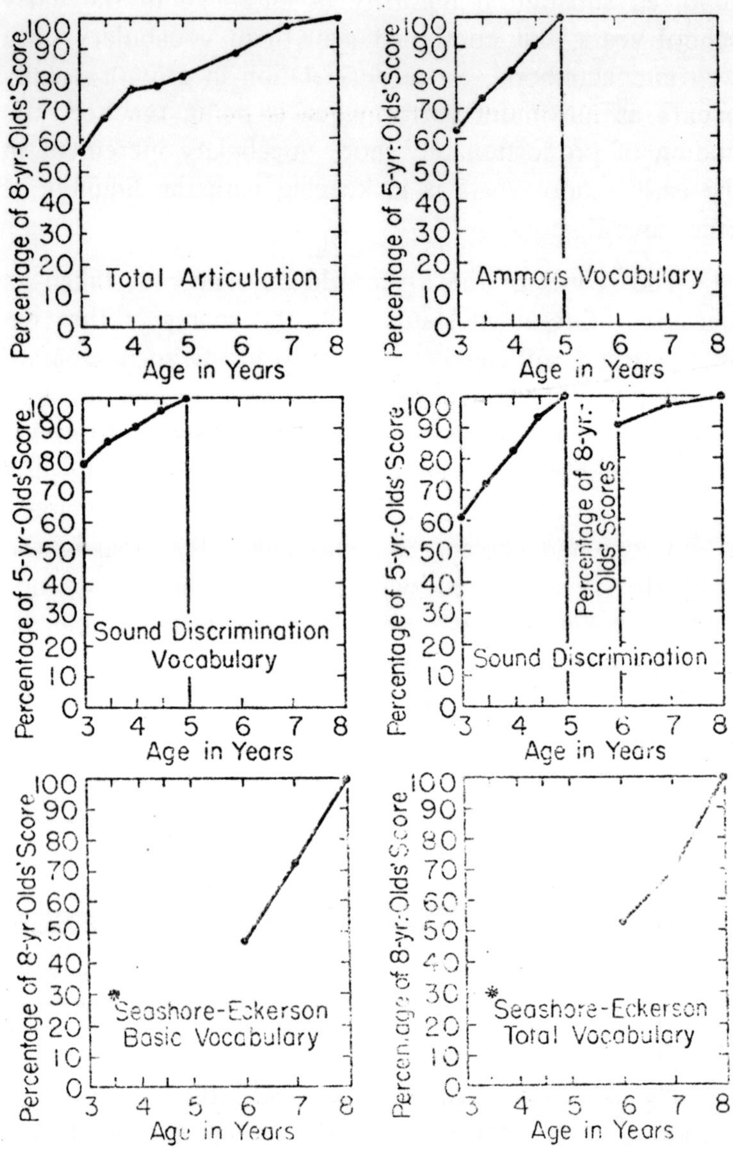

Percentage by a boy age of the use of the 8-year-old subsample taxen as a measure of terminal status on measures

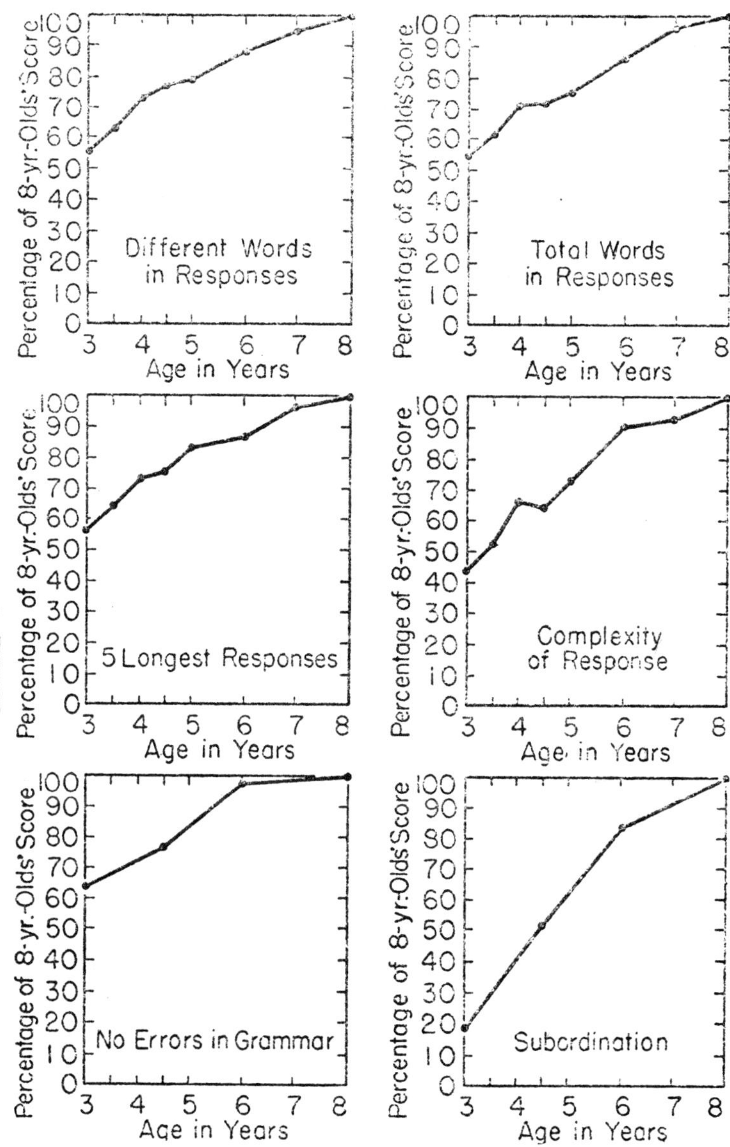

Percentage by a boy age of the use of the 8-year-old subsample taxen as a measure of terminal verbalisation measures

When the lowest age at which any test was used is considered in the comparison, the maximum range of differences is extended to 21.1 points with a mean of 8.7.

The greatest retardation of the LSES group is on the vocabulary scores. At 6 years the LSES group has reached about one third to two fifths of the scores of the 8-year-old USES group, while at 6 years the USES group has achieved somewhat over half the scores of the 8-year-old USES group. At this age only one score, "No grammatical errors," reaches 90 per cent of the terminal status measures. The others are all below 85 per cent of the attainment of the USES 8-year-olds. This is in sharp contrast to the picture presented by the two sexes where the scores of the boys on all the measures were at least 84 per cent of those of the 8-year-old girls. At 8 years of age the LSES group has achieved about three fourths that of the 8-year-old USES group. The LSES group does not reach the achievement of the 8-year-old USES group on any of the language variables.

Increments between consecutively tested age levels

In Table the *t* values of the differences between the achievement of the subsamples at consecutively tested age levels are summarized for the major language measures. It should be pointed out that only the differences between consecutively tested ages are considered. If such an increment is statistically significant, it is important. However, the lack of significance is not equally important when the development of youngsters is considered. Although increments between consecutively tested age levels are not statistically significant, the increments between more widely spaced age intervals may be. The trend of change is of psychological significance, and must be recognized.

Values showing significance of difference between consecutively tested age levels on major language measures

	CA						
Measure	3-3.5	3.5-4	4-4.5	4.5-6	5-6	6-7	7-8
Articulation							
Total articulation	2.96	2.46	0.51	0.98	2.48	2.63	1.93
Consonant elements	2.43	2.84	0.98	0.47	2.72	2.52	1.85
Double-consonant blends	2.91	2.25	0.32	1.15	2.27	2.42	2.00
Triple-consonant blends	.3.56	2.22	0.20	1.18	2.09	2.44	1.50
Vowels	0.17	0.08	0.00	0.09	0.33	0.17	0.00
Diphthongs	0.19	0.07	0.07	0.18	0.10	0.00	0.00
Nasals	1.55	1.57	0.38	0.81	1.67	1.88	1.00
Plosives	1.88	2.68	0.63	0.62	4.11	0.82	0.20
Fricatives	2.54	2.18	1.60	0.42	2.45	2.75	2.04
Combinations	1.96	3.15	0.93	0.31	1.24	0.13	0.17
Semivowels	1.63	2.59	0.07	0.68	2.11	1.72	0.11
Initial consonants	2.43	2.50	0.60	0.33	0.43	1.75	1.67
Final consonants	1.63	3.00	1.50	0.57	2.75	2.50	2.00
Initial double blends	2.60	4.28	0.44	1.55	2.75	2.15	1.83
Final reversed double blends	2.41	1.73	0.79	1.05	2.34	2.28	2.12
Initial triple blends	3.13	1.77	0.48	1.15	0.93	1.84	1.67
Final triple blends	2.73	0.52	0.52	1.58	0.46	1.77	0.87
Final reversed triple blends	3.45	2.43	0.94	0.94	3.02	3.11	1.27
Sound discrimination							
sound discrimination score						2.50	1.69
Sound discrimination Score C	2.88	3.64	2.94	1.91			
Vocabulary							
Number of different words	2.87	3.52	1.40	1.15	2.92	2.14	1.70
Sound discrimination vocabulary	2.83	2.52	3.07	1.33			
Ammons vocabulary	4.18	3.40	2.81	3.33			

Seashore-Eckerson basic (uncorrected)						4.97	5.21
Seashore-Eckerson basic						4.74	4.19
Seashore-Eckerson total (uncorrected)						3.17	4.76
Seashore-Eckerson total (corrected)						3.31	4.22
Verbalization							
Length of remark	2.72	3.14	0.15	1.20	3.23	3.26	1.27
5 longest remarks	2.91	3.31	0.51	1.76	1.00	3.04	1.26
One-word remarks	1.87	0.04	0.49	1.38	3.83	2.73	2.69
Complexity score	1.98	3.16	0.30	1.56	3.28	0.45	1.19

Of the 197 comparisons presented, in only 4 is there a reversal so that the younger age group receives the better score. For the one-word remarks the better score is the lower score, but for all other measures presented the better score is the higher one. Of course it is expected that over the age range studied, children will increase in the language abilities measured with an increase in age. However, the few small reversals which occurred indicate that the tests used and the sample selected were reasonably satisfactory.

One of the most interesting findings concerning these age trends is the substantial number of significant increments in all areas tested. Nearly half of all comparisons made reach at least the .05 level of confidence. In the language score between 3 and 3.5 years, the earliest ages tested, 19 of the 28 increments are significant at the .05 or .01 levels. Of those that are not statistically significant, three of the articulation measures—vowels, diphthongs, and nasals—have attained a high level of accuracy at 3 years of age and show no significant increments throughout the age range tested. Among the others, the four articulation scores show a significant increment between 3.5 and 4 years, the next older consecutively tested ages. The differences in the number of one-word remarks used at the several ages become significant only at the school ages.

A difference is apparent in the patterns of increment among the several language measures tested. the development of correct articulation, on the whole, shows most significant increments between consecutively tested age levels from 3 to 4 years and again from 5 to 7 years. No significant differences are found between 4 and 5 years. This could be a function of the particular sample tested, but this is a questionable explanation, since increments which are statistically significant do appear for the other language measures between these age levels. It is reasonable to find that accuracy in articulation increases substantially during the early preschool years when child language first begins to function as adult language, and again when children begin to attend school.

Sound discrimination shows significant increments throughout most of the preschool years and again between the youngest ages after school entry, despite different tests being used at the two ages. However, somewhat different patterns obtain for the preschool children when the picture sound discrimination test is scored using different scoring techniques. Using Score A, only the increment between 4.5 and 5 years reaches the .05 level. Using Score B the increment between 3.5 and 4 years reaches the .01 level and that between 4.5 and 5 years reaches the .05 level.

Throughout the range the measures of vocabulary of recognition show increments consistently significant at the .01 level. The measures of vocabulary of use are less consistent, but seven out of the eleven increments are significant at the .05 level or higher.

Among the verbalizations, the length and complexity of remarks show the greatest significant increments in the earliest years tested and in the early school years. The actual mean and median number of one-word remarks decreases substantially during the early preschool years. In the early school years, however, when the range of such performance becomes restricted, the decrements become statistically significant.

1. There is substantial interrelationship among the language skills measured, but the magnitude of the relationship varies with the skill measured.

2. The highest correlations are found between sound discrimination score and sound discrimination vocabulary. Intercorrelations among measures related to sentence structure are only slightly lower. On the whole, the correlations between vocabulary and the other language skills are of lower magnitude.

3. There are no marked age trends in the correlational pattern. However, there is a tendency for the intercorrelations among the verbalization measures and articulation to decrease with age. This is also true for sound discrimination and articulation over the entire age range; for sound discrimination and Ammons vocabulary scores from 3 to 5, and for either sound discrimination score and the verbalization scores from between 6 to 8. No consistent age trends occur either among the verbalization intercorrelations or between any of the language variables and intelligence.

5. With intelligence partialled out, the magnitude of the intercorrelations is somewhat reduced, although their rank order and the pattern of relation to age remains essentially the same, as was found for the zero order correlations.

6. With the achievement of the 8-year-old subsample taken as a measure of terminal status for those skills measured over the entire age range, the 3-year-olds have achieved about 50 per cent of the scores of the 8-year-olds in articulation, length of remark, and number of different words used; about 40 per cent in the complexity of verbalization; and about 20 per cent in the use of subordination.

7. When the achievement of the 8-year-old girls is taken as a measure, the growth patterns of boys and girls are similar and neither sex exhibits any consistent retardation.

8. When the achievement of the 8-year-old upper socioeconomic status group is taken as a measure of terminal status, the growth patterns of the upper socioeconomic status and the lower socioeconomic status groups are similar, and the lower socioeconomic status group is slightly retarded.

9. Nearly half of the increments in language scores obtained by consecutively tested age groups are statistically significant.

10. The several language skills measured show different patterns of increments. In articulation substantial growth occurs in the earliest years measured except in a few types of sounds in which a high level of accuracy of articulation has already been achieved by 3 years. With the exception of these, the articulation subscores show the most significant increments between 3 and 4 years and between 5 and 7 years. Sound discrimination scores and the length and complexity of verbalizations follow a similar pattern.

12

Initiatives in Teaching and Testing 'Language'

A new kind of language degree

It was at university level that the 'rethinking' called for by the Crowther Report began. The rapid expansion of universities in the 1960s gave the opportunity for several new approaches to language studies. It may be useful to describe one of those which was fairly typical of the new wave. This was the degree in 'language' created in York by the first head of the Language Department, Professor he Page, and his colleagues. Their task was made feasible by two decisions taken at an early stage in the academic planning of the new university. The first was to create a separate department for purely literary studies. The second decision was *not* to set up traditional schools of, for example, French or German but to subsume all foreign language degree work, as well as work in English *language*, in single department. This was the Language Department whose central core, common to all students, regardless of the language(s) in which they might specialise, was linguistics. A third decision, taken later, to cater for the obvious needs not met by the previously mentioned departments, was to create a department to serve a specialist function of teaching foreign languages, as well as to do research in foreign language acquisition and teaching methods, and to play a part in the training of graduate language teachers. This was the Language Teaching Centre.

Students in the York Language Department follow a four-year course. The first year is spent on an introduction to linguistics and on an intensive study, partly in the Language Teaching Centre, of the student's main European language. The second year is spent away from the university immersed in the French or German language. On this return to York at the beginning of the third year students face an oral test in their chosen language before embarking on the study of its history and structure in the remaining two year of the course. At the same time students are introduced to their second language, which must be either Chinese, Hindi or Swahili. The linguistic studies which predominate in the third and fourth years are informed and illustrated by the students' growing insight into the two contrasting languages chosen for study.

Though York language students read widely in the literature of their foreign language, as they must, in order to deepen their command of the idiom, at no time in their examinations or seminars are they required to make value judgments about the *literary* qualities of the works read, unless they deliberately choose an optional paper to be studied in the Department of English and Related Literatures.

The course is flexible, in that it may be combined wit other disciplines. Language and philosophy and language and education have been successful combinations. The York course has attracted students of the highest calibre from overseas. The best of these, while studying English as their specialism, are well placed, as native-speaking informants, to help their British fellow students in the study of languages such as Chinese, Hindi or Swahili.

The New York course has been described at some length because it represented, when the university opened in 1963, a radical break with the traditional approach both to English and to foreign language studies. Like other similarly radical courses elsewhere it has attracted sixth formers of high ability. The fact that, after 20 years, such a course no longer seems so revolutionary is a measure of the change that has taken place in expectations regarding language studies.

'Language" as a subject in the school curriculum

Bridging the space between L1 and L2

The sixth formers who applied to York and to other new courses did not wish to restrict their interest in language to literary criticism. They wanted to explore other equally important aspects of language, such as psycholinguistics or socio-linguistics. The success of the new university courses in 'language' naturally led to he question: Should not the school curriculum offer *all* pupils the opportunity to explore some of these issues, at an appropriate level? The synthesis between English and foreign language studies achieved at York was made possible because the new discipline of 'linguistics' bridged the gap that had traditionally separated the two. This led to a further question: Might study of 'language awareness' do the same in schools?

The possibility was first discussed publicly at a

national conference in Manchester in 1973, convened by George Perren, then director of the Centre for Information on Language Teaching. When he came to edit the conference papers for publication Perren took up a phrase introduced into the discussion by Jim Wight: 'the space between', referring to the different dialects met by pupils. Perren chose this as the title of the collected papers, giving it the wider sense of the space to be bridged between English and foreign languages and other ethnic minority mother tongues: 'all would be simpler in schools where no foreign languages were taught and where all children came with an acceptable form of English as their mother tongue. If rare today, such schools will be unknown in future'.

The possibility of building this kind of bridge had been raised specifically in one of the conference papers: 'I would see the subject as linking the two supporting studies of mother tongue and foreign language...which have hitherto, in nearly all schools, proceeded in completely separate departments'.

In later papers I have tried to develop to concept of the trivium comparing it with the medieval trivium on which famous grammar schools such as Winchester were based. The three elements of our proposed new trivium would reinforce each other in much the same way that the elements of the early Winchester syllabus did. The new element in the curriculum, 'awareness of language', would help pupils in their attack on the foreign language, by strengthening their capacity for 'insight into pattern' and setting up correct expectations as to what patterns to look for.

At the same time the foreign language in itself, if

properly presented, could help to develop pupils' awareness of language and combat linguistic parochialism. This required, of course, that the foreign language teaching strategies used must encourage pupils to compare their emerging insights in the new language with their intuitions about their mother tongue. A mere drilling in simple dialogues to meet hypothetical 'survival situations' could not contribute very much to language awareness, nor offer that apprenticeship in 'learning how to learn' languages on which later acquisition, by intensive means, of the language(s) of adult need could build.

A school shows the way

While the theorists were debating, the initiative of one enterprising school showed what was possible. In 1972 a new approach to language was introduced at Hessle High School, North Humberside. It was devised by Barry Laughton, head of modern languages there, who had already made his mark in the 1960s fir his imaginative use of the new techniques of 'group work' in language learning. He had the advice of Dr D. Reibel, then a member of the Language Department of York University, who visited the school several times, discussed the programme with Laughton and his colleagues and suggested reading and projects.

The general aims of the course were to give pupils an idea of language as a whole, its evolution, history and structure, to help them to appreciate the similarities between their own and other languages, 'so that they might feel closer to them', and at the same time to give them confidence in manipulating their own language.

The course, called a 'language foundation course', had as its immediate aims to enable pupils to make more informed choices between foreign languages offered during their secondary education and in part to compensate for what was felt to be the neglect , or underemphasis, of overt structure and grammar in the new 'audio-visual' methods then in vogue in the foreign language classroom. It occupied one school year, with 4 periods per week, in addition to, but separate from, the pupils' normal English lessons.

Laughton found that among the most popular items in the course, as revealed by the pupils' questionnaire, was the discussion of the baby learning to communicate, and that in most cases the pupils' families were interested in the course.

One of the significant aspects of this pioneering initiative was that, from the beginning, it was a team effort, planned jointly by the head of the school and the head of the lower school, the heads of the foreign language and the English departments and the two teachers who undertook the initial classroom work, one a Latinist and the other a Germanist.

Experiments along these lines, in introducing 'language' as a curriculum subject, have continued, at Hessle and elsewhere, with growing confidence.

Further initiatives by schools

After the publication of the Bullock Report interest in the kind of course pioneered at Hessle High School quickened. A number of schools began to experiment with language courses for pupils about to begin their secondary education. It is significant that in nearly every case it was the modern language staff who took the initiative. Some courses depended on individual initiative and did not survive when staff were promoted to other work.

An example of such a course which attracted wide interest, despite being short-lived, was the 'linguistics module' introduced at Archbishop Michael Ramsey's School, London, by the head of modern languages, David Cross. This was a team's work intercalated in each of years one and two, alongside the 'taster' introductions to languages other than French pioneered by this school. French study proper began in the third year only.

Henry box school

The language course developed at Henry Box School, Witney, Oxfordshire, became nationally known through the publication of the materials on which the course was based. This first-year course became incorporated into a longer-term treatment of language in the secondary curriculum, including the pioneering of a course of language in child-care pupils in the 15 to 16 age group which we discussed.. The first-year module itself was designed as a six- or seven-week introductory course for 11-year-olds about to start French. Experience has shown that the course has helped to create a more secure approach to the new language and at the same time to build a positive relationship between pupils and teacher. A summary of the course as designed in 1979 is as follows:

Aims

1 To create 'awareness of language'

2 To give practice in listening

3 To place the learning of a particular language in context

4 To create a positive relationship between pupils and teacher

Content

(i) *Language as communication*

(a) Definition

(b) Animal language

(c) Non-verbal communication

(d) Signs and signals

(e) Coded languages

(f) Speech

(g) Words

(ii) Acquisition of language

(a) How baby learns: follow progress of 0-5-year-old child with tape-recordings and video-cassettes, observing how the child develops linguistic ability

(b) Lessons to be drawn

  (i) importance of understanding before response

  (ii) necessity of making mistakes

  (iii) why is language acquisition so rapid and effortless?

(iii) Families of languages

(a) How many languages?

(b) Idea of language 'families'

(c) Most widely spoken ten international languages

(d) European languages

(e) Similarities between languages

(f) History of languages

(iv) Anatomy of language - Rules/Patterns

(a) Reference section - naming of parts

(b) Working together

(c) Differences between languages

(v) The golden rules

(a) Listen carefully

(b) Spot the Rules and Patterns

(c) Work hard in learning

(d) Make mistakes

(e) Watch for contacts

(f) Keep trying!

North westminster community school

An interesting comparison with the Henry Box course is offered by the World Languages Project developed in the Inner London Community School, North Westminster, a school with a large number of ethnic minorities in its catchment area.

This lower school foundation course was designed by the modern language staff of the school. It aims to prepare pupils for learning a future foreign language, either European or non-European, by overcoming prejudices and encouraging motivation. It is organised as follows:

Aims

1 To develop the language learning skills of speaking, reading and writing and to develop the skill of memorising

2 To strengthen awareness of grammatical concepts

3 To give an introduction to language variety, the development of languages and their interdependence

4 To encourage the comparison of structure, vocabulary and writing systems across languages

5 To break down intolerance and develop curiosity about language

6 To complement literacy skills in other subjects

The course attempts to achieve these aims as far as possible through direct experience of several languages.

Content

Years 1 and 2: Pupils study each of the main languages French, Spanish and German for 10 weeks each. In addition they do one 'short unit' each term of 2 weeks' duration. These include several non-European languages and a unit on language awareness.

Year3: Pupils embark on the study of their main language. They continue with the 'short units' as in years 1 and 2.

In the short units include Arabic, he Hebrew alphabet, the development of speech, the history of writing, Bahasa Indonesia, Bengali, language families, invented languages, Russian. It is envisaged that further units will soon be incorporated.

In the teaching of the main languages, links are made as far as possible with the short units. The latter are placed deliberately at points where useful comparisons can be made, for example, in year 2 to verb system of Bahasa Indonesia is compared with those of French, Spanish and German. In Year 1 the Hebrew and Russian alphabets and study of the history of writing providing support and comparison in tackling reading skills in Spanish and German.

One teacher takes the class for the whole programme in order to ensure that the links and comparisons are made and that progress can be continuously monitored.

Language in a child-care course

While at Banbury School, Peter Downes developed, with Paul Baker of the Banbury Teachers; Centre, a course is language for child-care groups of pupils in their fifth year. This course was further developed and modified at Henry Box School, as part of the follow-up to the Introduction to Language module offered to the first years. The course was later introduced at Hinchingbrooke School, Cambridgeshire. It is organised as follows:

Aims

1 To create an interest in the language of young children

2 To develop a basic understanding of the way children learn to talk

3 To give opportunities for the practice of techniques in talking to children

The course attempts to keep direct instruction and transmission of factual or theoretical knowledge to a minimum, relying some on observation of children, on role-play, discussion and playing with children.

Content

(i) introduction to the acquisition of language and the crucial role of parents and other adults

(ii) observation of a child aged between 2 and 3 playing with teacher/parent in the classroom followed by simple analysis in the group

(iii) study of the stages of language development up to the age of 5 with help of tape-recordings, stressing variation from the average as no cause for anxiety

(iv) study of examples of parental interaction with children and their effects using recordings; practical role-play of use of everyday situations to develop language

(v) practical activities showing how language develops through play and how inexpensive toys can be used in promoting language development

(vi) language of control: discussion of the various ways of controlling children; role-play of alternative approaches

(vii) recollection of the rhymes, songs, stories learned by the pupils as children and discussion of their use in language learning

(viii) use of examples of picture books and simple readers brought into the class by pupils and discussion of their use of widening vocabulary and stimulating conversation

(ix) discussion of television output for the under-fives with recorded examples: emphasis on value of parents and children watching and listening together and talking about the ideas put over; teaching the use of the OFF switch!

(x) discussion of implications of the course: value of stable home relationship; the need for 'adult time'; social and financial implications; effect of size of family; role and responsibility of father

Some interesting lessons have already been learnt from this work. It has been found that watching films and listening to broadcasts are not helpful. It is better for teachers to select examples from broadcasts to develop in discussion. The experiment of pupils trying to use small tape-recorders to record children's language took far too long and did not work except with exceptionally able pupils. Pupils also found it very hard to observe children in playgroups and to report back. They did not know what they were meant to be listening for unless given specific guidance.

Downes sees a number of problems that might arise in a course of this kind:

(a) There is the danger, since child-care groups tend to consist of girls, of implying that fathers do not have an important role in language development - the father's role needs to be stressed.

(b) Pupils do not retain linguistic theory and the use of linguistic terminology can be counter-productive.

(c) Pupils are brought by the course to think about its relevance to their own experience at home; great sensitivity is, therefore, called for and the teacher must know the pupils, and their backgrounds, well.

(d) An initial reaction can be that pupils believe the aim of the course is to make babies 'talk-posh', and this calls for sensitivity and perceptiveness in teaching.

(e) There is a danger of thinking of language as divorced from other activities; the role of language as divorced from other activities; the role of language as the key to relationships and other activities must be emphasised.

Both in its imaginative sweep and in the sensitivity with which it is presented this course deserves to be a model for any school which seeks to prepare future young parents for their demanding role.

The success of the courses at Banbury, Henry Box and Hinchingbrooke cannot fail to influence the development of child-care courses and points the way to the introduction of the essential language element that hitherto they have lacked.

New materials for language teaching

The production of new language-teaching materials, meanwhile, both helped to focus the theorists' debate and to encourage schools to follow the example of pioneers such as Hessle High school.

Basic linguistics for secondary schools

First in the field, by some years, was B.N. Ball, a lecturer at Doncaster College of Education, whose three-volume textbook *Basic Linguistics for Secondary Schools* appeared as early as 1967. This was an imaginative programme, to cover the middle three years of the secondary course and designed for average and less-than-average attainers.

It is probably impossible to quote an extract without being unfair to the course as a whole but the following may give some of the flavour of the material.

'Loaded' words

In Books 1 and 2 we saw that words themselves can be powerful. Skilled writers employed to sell commercial products know this. One extremely successful advertising man once drew up a list of the twenty most powerful words that could be used to sell goods. *NEW* and *FREE* were both high on the list.

How are these words powerful? do you recall seeing them used in advertisements? How are words usually printed or spoken - are they made to stand out from the background of the advertisement?

What other words are also used in this way?

The people who write advertisements use a practice of language that is common. We can see it at work in this piece of conversation:

'I hear your Fred's in hospital.'

'Yes.'

'What's the matter, then?'

'He's gone for psychiatric treatment.'

'The mental hospital!'

'Oh, he's not mad or anything like that. Don't go running away with the idea he's a nute-case!'

The words *psychiatric, mental, mad,* and *nut-case* are all concerned more or less with the same idea. Which are the 'loaded' words, in the sense that *NEW* and *FREE* were discussed as 'loaded'? What difference in meaning exists between these words? Why was the second speaker anxious to avoid the implications of some of them?

In another idea, where again there is much fear and prejudice, there are various words in English that describe people whose skin pigmentation is not the pale colour of the Anglo-Saxon race. Probably the most 'loaded' of all such words is *black*. Why is this?

What other words of this kind exist?

Which are meant to be deliberately offensive?

Which are accurate as words describing these peoples?

Are there any words used to describe people with the skin pigmentation of the Anglo-Saxon peoples? Who uses them?

Are any meant to be deliberately offensive?

How are 'loaded' words concerned with colour avoided by speakers who do not wish to give offence?

Finally, there are 'loaded' words which are used - particularly at election times - by the political parties. Which are meant to harm an opposing party?

Exercises

1 Examine the pages of newspapers and magazines, hoardings, and television commercials. Complete the list of twenty 'loaded' words that are most used by advertisers. List them in order of effectiveness.

2 Some of the following are known by other words. Make a list of all the other terms, in descending order of politeness:

   (a) private detective

   (b) hire-purchase

   (c) a patient undergoing psychiatric treatment

   (d) an employee who refuses to join other employees in a strike

   (e) a public-house

Explain how any one of (a) to (e) consists of 'loaded' words when a certain point is reached in the descending order of politeness.

3 Some of the most abusive language that appears in the daily news consists of exchanges between countries who resent one another's policies. Collect examples from news broadcasts and from newspapers, where a country, or its leaders, are referred to in uncomplimentary terms. Explain how any speaker of these examples uses 'loaded' words to attack the persons or country he is talking about.

Language in use

The Schools Council programme worked out by the team of Doughty, Pearce and Thornton under the chairmanship of Professor Halliday, and published in 1971, broke quite new ground. Whereas Ball had offered an approach to 'linguistics' appropriate for secondary school pupils, Halliday, in his introduction to *Language in Use*, came close to arguing for the kind of 'awareness of language' approach that we are advocating:

Each one of us has this ability and lives by it; but we do not always become aware of it or realise fully the breadth and depth of its possibilities...There is no place for language in the division of knowledge into arts and sciences—this is no doubt a principal reason for its neglect in our educational system, which depends on boundaries of this kind...There should, however, he some place for language in the working life of the secondary school pupil; and, it might be added, of the student in a College of Education.

The units of work in the Schools Council programme are grouped into three main aspects of language use:

(i) the nature and function of language

(ii) its place in the lives of individuals

(iii) its role in making human society possible

The aim of the units is: 'to develop in pupils and students awareness of what language is and how it is used and, at the same time, to extend their competence in using it'. The authors thys accept that 'awareness and competence are linked'. The material in *Language in Use* is not offered as a course to be worked through but rather as a resource bank from which each teacher will select units to suit pupils' interests.

Alpine

The set of teaching materials which came to be known as ALPINE was produced by a working party of teacher trainers and teachers based in Norwich which began work in 1975. The convenor of the group was the county language adviser, Ray Whiley. The acronym stands for 'A Language Project In Norfolk Education'. The ALPINE materials have not been published nationally but are disturbed within in LEA schools.

The Norfolk initiative was originally, in part, a reaction to the set-back to primary French. After the publication of the NFER Report *Primary French in the Balance* it was felt useful to rethink the place of language education for the 10 to 12 age group. A set of worksheets was produced offering materials for a one-year course conceived as an alternative to beginning French. Some schools, however, have used the materials with pupils who have started French, so that the two studies run in parallel.

The multimedia materials, which it was hoped teachers would not treat as a course but use to build their own courses to suit their and their pupils' interests, were divided into units of work and grouped in four areas:

(i) language as system

(ii) language in action

(iii) language across cultures

(iv) language as change

Support from teacher trainers

At teacher training level interest in 'awareness of language' in the curriculum has grown rapidly. Initiatives in promoting discussion of the new courses have mainly been taken by tutors in modern languages. Teacher training institutions which have already made significant contributions to the development of this area of the curriculum include: King's College London, Department of Education; Darham University, Department of Education; Ealing College of Higher Education; King Alfred's College, Winchester; Homerton College, Cambridge; Brighton Polytechnic; Department of English, University of Birmingham; Language Teaching Centre, University of York.

Although tutors in modern languages have been most active, specialists in English studies have also shown a growing interest in this development in the language curriculum. Teacher trainers who have travelled, in countries such as the United States and Australia, have become aware of the extent to which, in those countries, the kind of curriculum development we are advocating has, for over a decade, been actively discussed and developed in many schools.

The national congress on languages in education

NCLE was set up in 1976. It was the outcome of several years of discussions among some 40 national associations concerned with English, linguistics and foreign language teaching at school, university and polytechnic levels. Its purpose was to fill an obvious gap. There existed no national forum where teachers, researchers, examiners, advisers, publishers and others interested in all aspects of language in education could meet and discuss their common problems. The Congress seeks to meet this need through its working parties and its biennial assemblies The assemblies are prepared for by detailed discussion in working parties. These publish their discussion documents for consideration by the constituent associations prior to each assembly. At the first assembly of the Congress in 1978. at Durham, I was invited to write a paper on 'Language as a Curriculum Study'. Summing up the argument of my paper I suggested that: 'study of language in the curriculum could be the place where mother tongue acquisition makes contact with foreign languages and with the languages of immigrants. As it is there is no meeting ground.'

The followed, at the next assembly, a working-party report, *Issues in Language Education*, 'Language Policies in Schools with Special Reference to Co-operation Between Teachers of Foreign Languages and Teachers of English'. The working party found very little evidence that the approach which had come to be called 'language across the curriculum', following Bullock, had made any headway at all in schools. While the 1980 working party reported that they could not come to an agreed policy about the alternative strategy to Bullock, namely offering 'language' as a curriculum subject, they did recommended that carefully monitored experiments in this direction would be justified.

According the standing committee of NCLE set up in 1980 a small working group chaired by John Trim, director of CILT, who was succeeded in the following year by Professor John Sinclair of Birmingham University, to co-ordinate and monitor the pilot schemes in 'awareness of language' which by now were proliferating in the schools. The first task of the group was to summon a national conference in Birmingham in January 1981. Here it was decided to attempt to map the variety of new courses their degree of success.

The third Assembly of NCLE, held in 1982, authorised the working group of proceed to the next stage of its work: the close observation by members of the group of the most interesting of the experiments, followed by their description in a series of case studies. These would be valuable in assessing the extent to which the experiments were fulfiling their stated aims and would facilitate the production of teaching materials and the planning of initial and in service training courses. It was hoped that the schools might also gain from making contact with other pioneering schools, and by widening their own experience.

To lunch his stage of its work the working group convened a second national conference at Leeds University in January 1983 at which six schools which had made particular progress in developing 'awareness of language' in the curriculum gave accounts of their work. A full account of the expansion of such programmes, with case studies of selected schools' initiatives, can be found in the proceedings of the 4th Assembly of NCLE.

Index